BLOOM

IN ANY SEASON

52 Ways to Grow into Your Magical Self

Dr. Makeba Morgan Hill

For more information, email drmakeba@drmakeba4love.com

Paperback ISBN: 979-8-9921007-5-4
Cover Art by: ThriveIn Learning Institute
Edited by: ThriveIn Learning Institute

Printed in the United States of America

Dedication

For the dreamers, the seekers, and the souls waiting to bloom, this book is for you. May you discover the magic within, trust your own unfolding, and remember that you are love, you are light, and you are infinitely blessed.

Table of Contents

Introduction

"If you seek love within first, you will never be without."
- Dr. Makeba Morgan Hill

I thought I had figured it all out. I had a great career, earning good money as a corporate executive. I was married, with a daughter, a cat, a dog, and a big, beautiful house. I earned a doctorate in higher education administration. I traveled the world. On paper, everything seemed perfect. I was living what appeared to be the American dream. But something was missing, and I couldn't quite put my finger on what it was.

We're often told our value comes from our achievements, the roles we play, and the recognition we get from the world. In chasing these, it's easy to lose touch with our inner selves—the parts of us that need love and acceptance the most. I did all the things I was "supposed" to do. I worked hard, cared for my family, and ensured everyone had what they needed. I had perfected the art of being there for everyone else, except for the one person I had been neglecting: me.

The truth is, I was living for everyone else except myself. I hadn't really taken the time to look in the mirror and ask if I was truly happy, if I was whole, if I was living or just managing —or even if it was okay to want more.

Does this sound familiar? Have you ever found yourself doing everything for everyone else, but leaving little time to care for you? Do you feel like something is missing, even though you've checked all the boxes for a successful life?

I had spent years striving, achieving, and living, but something deep inside me knew there was more to life than the roles I played and the boxes I checked. That's when I stumbled upon Reiki, a form of energy healing that works by channeling universal life force energy to promote physical, emotional, and spiritual well-being. It's a gentle but powerful practice that helps balance your energy and remove blockages that may be keeping you stuck. Reiki can bring deep healing, clarity, and a sense of peace.

It was during my Reiki Level 1 attunement—a sacred process that connects you to the flow of this healing energy—that everything shifted for me. It felt like a door opened wide, and I finally stepped into the fullness of who I was meant to be. I realized that up until that point, I had been waiting—waiting to bloom into my true self.

As my journey unfolded, it became clear to me that my purpose is to help others on this path of self-discovery and transformation. As a holistic coach and healer, my life's work is to help others remember who they are and why they are here. I am here to guide you in reconnecting with your inner self, embracing your unique magic, and living in alignment with your truth.

And here's the thing: Reiki was my path. You don't need a Reiki attunement to unlock the magic within you. You can become your full self through many different pathways. This book is simply one of the tools you can use on your journey—one that will guide, support, and help you bloom into who you're truly meant to be.

So, what does it mean to bloom? Blooming is more than growth—it's a full expression of who you are. It's about unfolding layer by layer, shedding the parts of yourself that no longer serve you, and stepping into your true power. When you bloom, you don't just exist—you thrive. Blooming is the moment when you embrace your magic, your light, and your full potential. When you bloom, you will live in alignment with your heart and soul.

How This Book Works

Bloom in Any Season: 52 Ways to Grow into Your Magical Self is designed as a yearlong guide to help you build a life anchored in self-love. The book is a gradual process, with inquiries and practices that deepen as the weeks go by, intentionally leading you into more soulful self-discovery and transformation. Early weeks lay the foundation, and as you move forward, the reflections and poetry become more intricate, reflecting the depth of your unfolding.

Each week, you will find:

- An Action Item: Practical steps to apply self-love and create positive shifts in your life. These action items build in complexity as you go, helping you develop deeper habits of self-care and spiritual connection.
- A Poem: To stir your soul and awaken your inner magic. The poetry will evolve from simple, rhythmic verses to more nuanced expressions, reflecting the journey toward your true self.
- An Affirmation: To keep your heart tuned to love's frequency. These affirmations guide you to embody love and joy as a natural state of being.
- An Intention Prompt: Each week begins with setting an intention, allowing you to consciously focus on how you want to grow, heal, or align with your inner truth. This practice anchors the energy of the week and gives you a powerful tool for transformation.
- A Reflection Prompt: This is a space for you to write down your thoughts, feelings, and discoveries along the way. It is here to deepen your self-awareness as you integrate these practices into your life.

At the end of the book, you'll also find a special tool: the Gardener's Log. Think of it as your personal record of growth and reflection throughout this journey. Each week, you'll have the opportunity to track your progress, revisit the affirmations and poems that resonated with you, and acknowledge the nurturing you've given yourself along the way. Every entry in the Gardener's Log celebrates your resilience, growth, and commitment to self-love. It serves as both a reference and a reminder of the care you've invested in tending your personal garden of transformation.

Just as a garden requires time, patience, and love to flourish, so does your self-love journey. The Gardener's Log is here to help you honor that process and keep track of your blooming progress.

Think of this book as your companion on the journey back to yourself. You don't have to rush. Take your time, move through the practices with intention, and let each week unfold as it should. This is a process of growth and evolution, and your journey will be unique to you.

What You'll Gain

By working through this book, you'll learn:
- How to cultivate self-love that is sustainable and transformative
- How to face obstacles with courage and resilience
- How to reconnect with your inner light and live with joy and fulfillment
- How to honor your own magic and bloom into the fullest version of yourself

This journey goes beyond simply checking off tasks—it's a path toward truly stepping into your power and becoming the magical person you're meant to be. I'll be right here with you, guiding and cheering you on each step of the way. Remember: You are love. You are light. You are blessed. Let's bloom together.

Section 1

Awaken the Magic Within
Discovering Self-Love

> *Learning to love yourself is the greatest love of all.*
> – Whitney Houston

Introduction

Welcome to the beginning of your journey toward embracing self-love. This is a sacred process of uncovering the true value that lies within you. It's time to peel back the layers of doubt, criticism, and comparison that have kept you from seeing your own worth. Before we can pour love into the world around us, we must first find and nurture it within ourselves.

Self-love is not just an act of kindness toward yourself—it's the foundation upon which a life filled with joy, respect, and fulfillment is built. The path you're about to walk will challenge you to see yourself differently to embrace the love that resides within you. Each step forward is a step toward your most powerful, authentic self. Remember, self-love isn't just another thing to do; it's a relationship to nurture, one day at a time.

Week 1: Identify Your Values

Planting the Seeds

This week, take time to sit quietly and reflect on what truly matters to you. Your values are the core of who you are. They guide your decisions and shape the life you live. Reflect on these questions:

- What values make you feel grounded and secure?
- When do you feel most aligned with your true self?
- Have you been living in accordance with your values, or have they been neglected?

Write down the top five values that resonate deeply with you. These might include honesty, compassion, creativity, independence, or service. Understanding your core values is the foundation of practicing self-love because it helps you make choices that reflect your truest self.

_____

_____

_____

_____

_____

_____

_____

_____

The Core of Me

In the quiet of my soul, I seek,
Through the noise and clamor, a peak
Into my heart, where my values lie clear,
Whispers of truth I hold dear.
Honesty, a beacon in the night,
Compassion, a guiding light,
Creativity, the soul's delight,
Independence, a flight of might.
These are the pillars of my core,
Now and forever more.

Set Your Intention

At the start of the week, set an intention to live in alignment with your values. How do you want your values to show up in your life this week? Choose one value to focus on and let it guide your actions.

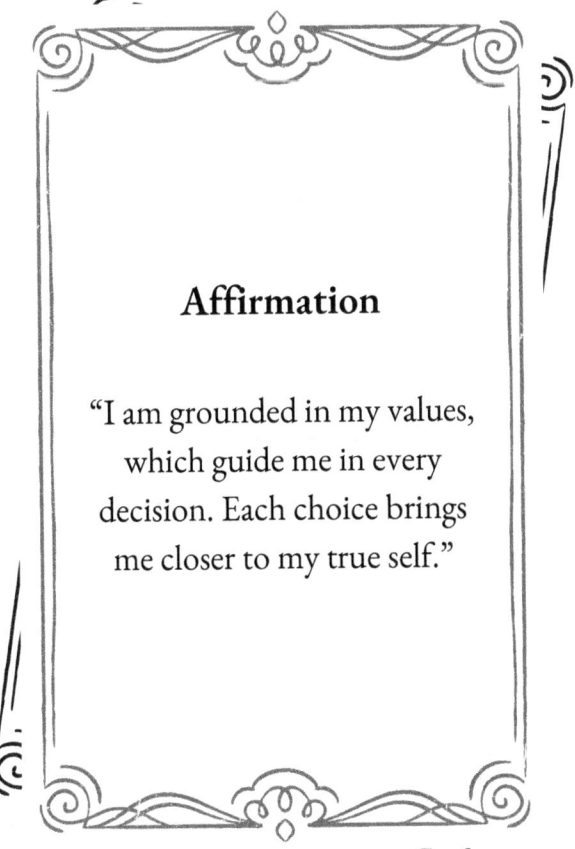

Affirmation

"I am grounded in my values, which guide me in every decision. Each choice brings me closer to my true self."

Reflection

At the end of the week, reflect on how your values influenced your decisions.

 Did you feel more aligned with your true self?

 Were there moments when it was difficult to stay true to your values?

Keep going—living in alignment with your values is a continuous journey toward self-love.

_____

_____

_____

_____

_____

_____

_____

_____

_____

_____

_____

_____

_____

_____

Week 2 : Set Healthy Boundaries

Planting the Seeds

Boundaries are an act of self-love. This week, reflect on where your energy is being drained and consider where you need to set healthier boundaries. Ask yourself:

- In which relationships or situations do I feel overextended?
- What can I say "no" to that will create space for myself?
- How can I communicate my boundaries clearly and lovingly?

Setting boundaries doesn't just protect your time and energy—it allows you to show up fully for yourself and others.

_____

_____

_____

_____

_____

_____

_____

_____

_____

_____

_____

_____

My Sacred Space

In the garden of my soul, I draw a line,
A boundary, clear and defined.
A space for me, where I can breathe,
In my sanctuary, I believe.
With each "no," a yes to self,
A declaration of my health.
In setting limits, I find peace,
In sacred space, my soul's release.

Set Your Intention

Before diving into the week, set an intention to honor yourself by setting boundaries. What area of your life will you focus on this week? Be clear with yourself about how you want to protect your energy.

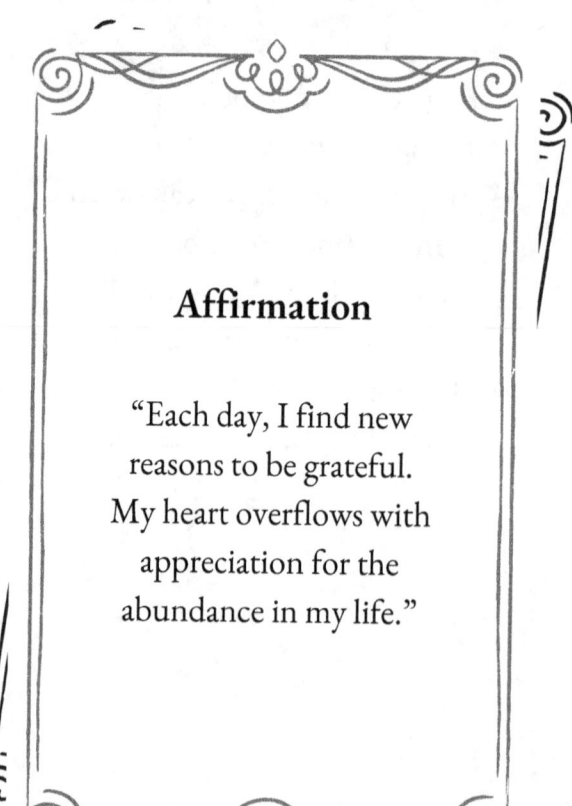

Affirmation

"Each day, I find new reasons to be grateful. My heart overflows with appreciation for the abundance in my life."

Reflection

Reflect on how it felt to set boundaries this week.
- Were you able to communicate them effectively?
- D id it get easier with practice?

Keep it up—each step you take toward honoring your limits strengthens your relationship with yourself.

Week 3: Cultivate Gratitude

Planting the Seeds

Gratitude is a powerful practice that shifts your focus from what's lacking to what's abundant in your life. This week, start a gratitude journal. Find gratitude in the mundane, and the extraordinary will become even more delicious. Consider these questions:

- What small joys bring you peace or happiness?
- Who or what are you most grateful for today?
- How can you cultivate gratitude, even on challenging days?

Write down three things each day that you are grateful for. Let this practice become a daily reminder of the beauty that surrounds you.

_____

_____

_____

_____

_____

_____

_____

_____

_____

_____

_____

Gratitude's Gentle Embrace

A gentle breeze whispers on my skin,
An embrace of warmth, where thanks begin.
In the quiet dawn, a soft light wakes,
Grateful for each breath I take.
The world unfolds in colors bright,
A canvas of wonder, pure delight.
In every moment, blessings flow,
Gratitude's touch in all I know.
With each step forward, joy takes flight,
Grateful for both day and night.
For in this life, through ebb and grace,
I find my heart in gratitude's embrace.

Set Your Intention

At the beginning of the week, set an intention to notice the small joys in your life. How will you cultivate gratitude throughout the week, even when it feels difficult?

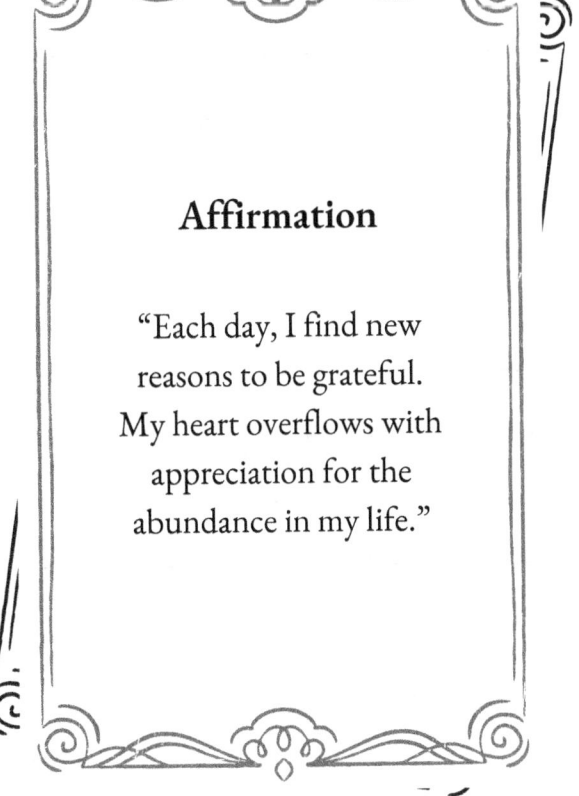

Affirmation

"Each day, I find new reasons to be grateful. My heart overflows with appreciation for the abundance in my life."

Reflection

Keep it up! Gratitude is essential for a joyful heart. Review your gratitude journal and reflect on how this practice shifted your perspective.

✦ Were there days when it was harder to find things to be grateful for? How
✦ did acknowledging gratitude impact your sense of peace?

Week 4 : Explore Your Creativity

Planting the Seeds

Creativity is a way to express the unique magic inside you. This week, carve out time to explore something creative without any pressure—paint, write, dance, cook, or simply create for the joy of it. Consider:

- When was the last time I created without worrying about the outcome?
- How can I bring more playfulness and creativity into my daily life?
- What happens when I let go of expectations and just let my creativity flow?

Allow yourself to enjoy the process, not just the end result.

_____

_____

_____

_____

_____

_____

_____

_____

_____

_____

_____

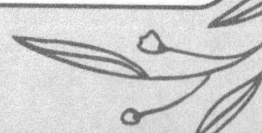

The Dance of Creativity

My pen ignites a spark within,
To move to the rhythm of my own drum.
Dance with me—choose your way,
A brush, a thread, whatever calls today.
Joy in every stroke, light in every play,
Creativity flows as we slay.
In this dance, we're free to explore,
Creating from our soul's core.

Set Your Intention

Set an intention to let your creativity flow
without limits. How will you allow
yourself to explore and express your
creative spirit this week?

Affirmation

"Creativity flows through me
effortlessly. I embrace my
artistic expressions with an
open heart and mind."

Reflection

 How did it feel to create freely this week?

Did letting go of expectations bring you joy or relief?

Keep nurturing your creativity—this allows you to connect with your inner world, release emotions, explore new perspectives, and cultivate joy.

_____

_____

_____

_____

_____

_____

_____

_____

_____

_____

_____

_____

_____

_____

_____

_____

Week 5 : Prioritize Your Health

Planting the Seeds

This week, focus on one way to show your body some love. Whether it's adding more water to your routine, eating better, or moving your body, make choices that honor your physical well-being. Ask yourself:

- What's one simple way I can show my body more love this week?
- Are there any small, daily habits I can build to support my health?
- How will nurturing my body help me feel more alive and connected?

Your body does so much for you—this is your time to return the favor.

A Vow to My Body

To my body, a temple, a treasure so rare,
A vow of health, a promise to care.
With nourishment pure and movement divine,
In wellness and strength, together we'll shine.
For each healthy choice, a step toward grace,
A journey of love, at my own pace.
In honoring health, I find my power,
In the temple of self, my spirit flowers.

Set Your Intention

At the start of the week, set an intention to make choices that honor your body. What one area of your physical health will you focus on?

Affirmation

"I honor my body with choices that promote health and vitality. My commitment to my well-being is an act of self-love."

Reflection

✦ How did your body respond to the care you gave it this week?
✦ Did making healthier choices impact your energy or mood?
Keep tuning in—your body deserves love and care every day.

_____

_____

_____

_____

_____

_____

_____

_____

_____

_____

_____

_____

_____

_____

_____

_____

Week 6 : Practice Mindfulness

Planting the Seeds

Mindfulness means being fully present. This week, set aside at least five minutes a day to practice. Some of the things you can try are mindful walking, mindful breathing, or mindful listening. Focus on your breath, and when thoughts come, gently bring your attention back to the moment. Ask yourself:

- How often do I feel fully present in my life?
- What helps me stay grounded when I'm feeling scattered or stressed?
- How can I create little moments of mindfulness throughout my day?

Mindfulness helps you slow down and connect with yourself in a deeper way.

_____

_____

_____

_____

_____

_____

_____

_____

_____

_____

In This Moment

In the stillness, I find my breath,
Sometimes it feels like a test.
But here, in this pause, I reclaim my peace,
Letting anxious thoughts slowly cease.
Each inhale grounds me, steady and true,
Each exhale whispers, "I'll carry you through."
In this moment, I find my grace,
Present with life, I take my place.

Set Your Intention

At the beginning of the week, set an intention to stay present. How will you remind yourself to come back to the present moment when life feels overwhelming?

Affirmation

"With each breath, I anchor myself in the present moment. I embrace mindfulness as a way to feel calm and centered."

Reflection

 How did practicing mindfulness affect your week?

 Were you able to stay grounded in the moment more often?

Mindfulness helps you feel more connected to yourself and to life. Make it a habit to practice mindfulness more often in the coming weeks.

_____

_____

_____

_____

_____

_____

_____

_____

_____

_____

_____

_____

_____

_____

_____

Week 7 : Deepen Your Sleep Ritual

Planting the Seeds

How many hours of sleep do you get each day? Sleep is vital for your mind, body, and soul. This week, focus on creating a nighttime routine that helps you wind down and rest deeply. Turn off screens, dim the lights, and do something calming before bed. Ask yourself:

- How can I make bedtime more peaceful and relaxing?
- What changes can I make to improve my sleep quality?
- How does better rest impact my energy and mood the next day?

Good sleep is one of the best gifts you can give yourself.

The Night's Embrace

As twilight deepens and stars ignite the sky,
I prepare to rest, letting the day pass by.
With soothing rituals, the noise fades away,
In the quiet of the night, my soul learns to stay.
The silence wraps me, gentle and warm,
Beneath the soft glow of the silvery moon's charm.
In sleep, I find strength; in stillness, I heal,
Embraced by the night, my peace becomes real.

Set Your Intention

Set an intention to prioritize your rest this
week. How will you make sure that your
bedtime routine helps you relax and
prepare for deep sleep?

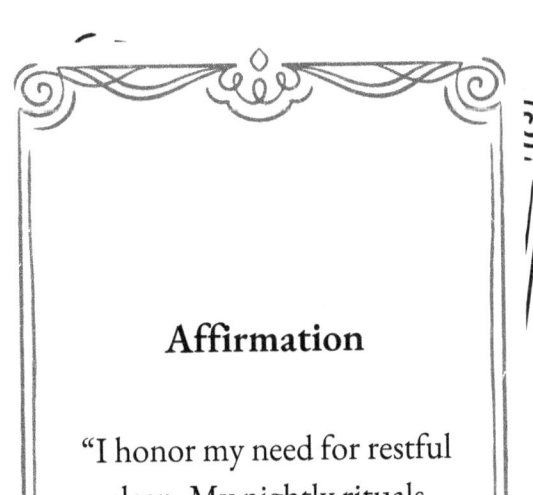

Affirmation

"I honor my need for restful
sleep. My nightly rituals
nurture my body and soul,
helping me wake up refreshed."

Reflection

✦ How did your sleep change this week?
✦ Did creating a bedtime routine help you rest more deeply?
Make it a habit to honor your sleep time—the foundation for a vibrant life.

_____

_____

_____

_____

_____

_____

_____

_____

_____

_____

_____

_____

_____

_____

Week 8 : Connect with Nature

Planting the Seeds

Nature has a way of grounding and restoring us. This week, spend time outside —whether it's a walk in the park, gardening, or simply sitting by a tree. Let yourself be fully present in the natural world. Consider:

- When was the last time I let nature heal me?
- How can I make time to connect with nature, even in small ways?
- How does being in nature shift my energy and mood?

Let the earth's rhythm guide you back to yourself.

Nature's Caress

Amid the whispering trees, I roam,
Under the sky, I find my home.
With every leaf, with every stone,
In nature's caress, I'm never alone.

Set Your Intention

At the start of the week, set an intention to
let nature ground and uplift you. How
will you spend time outdoors, letting the
natural world support your well-being?

Affirmation

"I find harmony and peace in
nature's embrace. Connecting
with the earth grounds me and
fills my soul with joy."

Reflection

-  How did spending time in nature affect your mood and energy?
- Did you notice any shifts in how you felt after being outdoors?

Keep this connection—Mother Nature has a way of bringing us back to ourselves

_____

_____

_____

_____

_____

_____

_____

_____

_____

_____

_____

_____

_____

_____

_____

Week 9 : Foster New Connections

Planting the Seeds

We are meant to connect to others. This week, make an effort to reach out to someone new or deepen a relationship. Whether it's reaching out to an old friend or introducing yourself to someone new, nurture meaningful connections. Reflect on:

- Who can I reach out to this week to reconnect or get to know better?
- How can I be more open to new connections in my life?
- What do I value most in the relationships I already have?

Each connection brings a new dimension to your life and your self-love journey.

Bridges Between Hearts

Between us, a bridge begins to grow,
With words unspoken but hearts that know.
A thread of light in every smile,
Connecting souls across the miles.
In the sharing of truth, our spirits rise,
In every connection, a new world lies.
With each new bond, a story unfolds,
And in these moments, our hearts are whole.

Set Your Intention

Set an intention to foster connections
this week. Will you deepen an existing
relationship or open yourself up to
new ones?

Affirmation

"I open my heart to meaningful
connections, knowing each
person I meet reflects a part of
me. Building bridges enriches
my life and nourishes my soul."

Reflection

◆ How did it feel to foster or deepen connections this week?
◆ Did reaching out make you feel more connected and supported?
Keep nurturing relationships—more people need to experience your light.

_____

_____

_____

_____

_____

_____

_____

_____

_____

_____

_____

_____

_____

_____

_____

_____

Week 10 : Practice Self-Compassion

Planting the Seeds

We often show compassion to others but forget to extend it to ourselves. This week, practice self-compassion by being gentle with yourself in difficult moments. Reflect on:

- How do I speak to myself when I make a mistake or face challenges?
- What can I say or do to be kinder to myself?
- How can self-compassion help me grow, rather than be hard on myself?

Self-compassion is an act of love that helps you heal and grow.

_____

_____

_____

_____

_____

_____

_____

_____

_____

_____

_____

The Voice of Compassion

I whisper grace in the face of pain.
A quiet breath, a soft refrain.
Within my heart, I hold the key,
To offer love and dignity.
No blame, no shame, just tender care,
I choose compassion, light as air.
In kindness, I reclaim my way,
Loving myself through every day.

Set Your Intention

Set an intention to practice self-compassion this week. How will you offer yourself kindness in moments of difficulty or self-doubt?

Affirmation

"I treat myself with kindness and compassion. I offer myself grace and understanding as I navigate life's challenges."

Reflection

✦ How did self-compassion change your inner dialogue this week?

✦ Did being kinder to yourself help you feel more supported?

Keep practicing self-compassion—it's how you heal from the inside out. By offering yourself grace, you soften the edges, embrace your imperfections, and allow love to flow where self-judgment once stood. This is how you build a deeper, more authentic relationship with yourself—one rooted in kindness and acceptance.

_____

_____

_____

_____

_____

_____

_____

_____

_____

_____

_____

_____

_____

_____

Week 11 : Practice Forgiveness

Planting the Seeds

Forgiveness is one of the most essential ways to free yourself. This week, focus on letting go of old grudges toward yourself and others. Reflect on:

- Where am I holding onto resentment or guilt that I can release?
- How can forgiveness create more space for love and joy in my life?
- What does it feel like to forgive myself for past mistakes?

Forgiveness is a gift you give yourself.

The Path to Forgiveness

A burden carried, heavy and tight,
In chains of the past, blocking the light.
But within my grasp, a key to release,
Forgiveness, the doorway to inner peace.
To forgive is not to erase or forget,
But to heal, to let go of lingering regret.
A lightness, a freedom, a new day begins,
On the path of forgiveness, my spirit wins.

Set Your Intention

Set an intention to practice forgiveness
this week. How will releasing old hurts
help you open up to more peace and love?

Affirmation

"I choose forgiveness, freeing
myself and others from the
past. In forgiveness, I find peace
and the strength to heal and
move forward."

Reflection

- How did forgiveness feel this week?
- Did letting go bring a sense of relief or lightness?

Did you have a hard time with this one? Many people often do. Keep practicing —it frees your heart and helps you live more peacefully.

_____

_____

_____

_____

_____

_____

_____

_____

_____

_____

_____

_____

_____

_____

_____

_____

Week 12 : Pause for Self-Reflection

Planting the Seeds

Self-reflection helps you pause, check in with yourself, and take stock of where you are on your journey. This week, dedicate time each day to reflect on your thoughts, feelings, and experiences. Consider:

- What have I learned about myself over the past weeks?
- Are there areas of my life where I feel more aligned with my true self?
- How can I further deepen my connection to myself?

When we take time to reflect, we open the door to deeper understanding and create space for more growth.

_____

_____

_____

_____

_____

_____

_____

_____

_____

_____

_____

_____

The Mirror Within

Quiet moments invite me near,
The parts of self, becoming clear.
With every glance, the truth appears,
A path of wisdom through the years.
The mirror shows what I once denied,
Now I walk with love and pride.
Through reflection, I start to see,
The depth of who I've come to be.

Set Your Intention

Set an intention to reflect on your journey
this week. How will self-reflection help
you gain more clarity and self-awareness?

Affirmation

"I pause for self-reflection,
honoring the growth and
wisdom I uncover within. Each
moment of introspection
brings me closer to my true
self."

Reflection

Take time this week to journal about the insights that arise during your self-reflection.

 What new discoveries have you made about yourself?

How does reflecting on your journey enhance your understanding of where you are and where you're headed?

_____

_____

_____

_____

_____

_____

_____

_____

_____

_____

_____

_____

_____

_____

Week 13 : Take Time to Celebrate Wins

Planting the Seeds

Celebrating your progress, no matter how big or small, is an essential part of self-love. This week, take time to recognize and honor your achievements. It could be something as simple as making it through a tough week or hitting a major milestone. Reflect on:

- What accomplishments, both big and small, have I achieved lately?
- How can I take a moment to celebrate myself today?
- How do I feel when I take time to recognize my efforts?

Celebrate yourself—you've come further than you realize.

_____

_____

_____

_____

_____

_____

_____

_____

_____

A Celebration of Me

In moments of triumph, great and small,
I rise and honor each step, each call.
For in the journey, I find my strength,
Through every challenge, I go the length.
No win too small, no joy too light,
I celebrate me, in day and night.
In each success, I find my power,
Blooming in joy, like a radiant flower.

Set Your Intention

At the beginning of this week, set an intention to celebrate your wins. How will you honor your progress and take time to acknowledge the growth you've achieved?

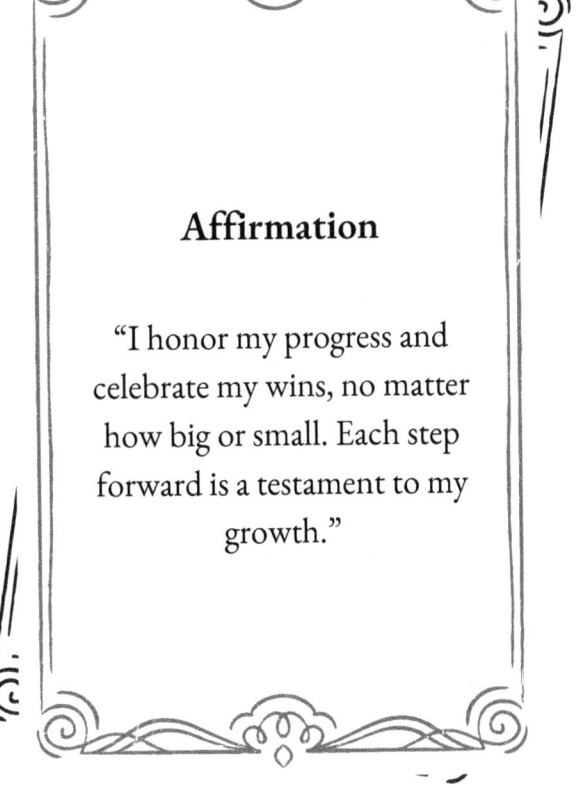

Affirmation

"I honor my progress and celebrate my wins, no matter how big or small. Each step forward is a testament to my growth."

Reflection

✦ How did taking time to celebrate your wins impact you this week?

✦ Did recognizing your accomplishments make you feel more empowered? Keep celebrating—you deserve to acknowledge the growth and progress you've made.

_____

_____

_____

_____

_____

_____

_____

_____

_____

_____

_____

_____

_____

_____

_____

_____

Section 2

Live in Your Light
Practicing Self-Love Daily

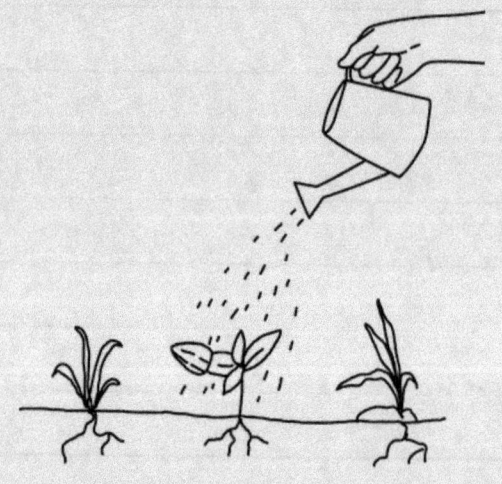

> *Doing the best at this moment puts you in the best place for the next moment.* - Oprah

Introduction

The best way to discover your true self is to dedicate quality time to loving on beautiful you. Building self-love is a practice, one that requires time, patience, and consistency. Much like strengthening a muscle, it takes dedication and daily attention. This doesn't have to be complicated. This section will guide you toward integrating self-love into the moments that make up your day. You'll see that you begin to flourish when you take small, mindful actions like speaking to yourself with compassion, making better choices, and carving out time for personal care.

For me, there were times when weaving self-love into my daily routine felt difficult. Life is busy, and it's easy to put yourself last. But I realized that the small acts matter just as much as the big ones. Drinking a cup of tea with full awareness, taking a moment to breathe deeply, or dedicating a few minutes to reflect each morning can transform your well-being.

In the weeks ahead, you'll explore ways to practice self-love daily. From setting intentions to nourishing your body, each practice will help you create a life where self-love isn't just an occasional indulgence—it's a regular part of your day. Remember, perfection is not the objective; it's about showing up for yourself every day in ways that feel meaningful and aligned with your growth.

Week 14 : Begin Your Day with Intention

Nurturing the Growth

Each morning, take a few minutes before diving into your day to set an intention. Whether it's an emotion you want to cultivate (such as peace or joy) or a specific goal you want to focus on, allow this intention to guide your actions throughout the day. Take a deep breath, reflect, and choose a meaningful direction for your day. Consider:

- How do I want to feel today?
- What can I focus on today that will bring me closer to my goals?
- How can I align my actions with my deeper values?

_____

_____

_____

_____

_____

_____

_____

_____

_____

_____

_____

_____

Dawn's Promise

As dawn's first light begins to rise,
I set my gaze toward the skies.
A quiet promise to live with grace,
To greet each moment I will face.
With intention clear, I carve my way,
Guided by purpose through the day.
This vow to self, a sacred start,
A journey forward, led by heart.

Set Your Intention

At the start of each day this week, pause
and set an intention. What do you want to
accomplish, or how do you want to feel?
Let this guide your day.

Affirmation

"Each morning, I set my
intention, guiding my actions
and thoughts throughout the
day. My intention shapes my
reality and aligns with my inner
truth."

Reflection

✦ How did setting an intention each morning change how you approached your day?

✦ Did you feel more grounded or purposeful?

Reflect on any shifts you noticed in your mood or actions. How will you incorporate this in the future?

_____

_____

_____

_____

_____

_____

_____

_____

_____

_____

_____

_____

_____

_____

Week 15:
Deepen Your Relationship with Food

Nurturing the Growth

This week, focus on building a deeper relationship with food. Instead of just eating mindfully, explore how food makes you feel energetically and emotionally. Take note of what foods make you feel vibrant, grounded, or sluggish. Try different types of foods and be open to new experiences that support your overall well-being. Consider:

- How do different foods affect my energy levels and emotions?
- Am I eating out of habit or hunger?
- What foods bring me joy and nourishment?

_____

_____

_____

_____

_____

_____

_____

_____

_____

_____

A Meal, A Moment

With every bite, I taste life's delight,
Flavors rich, bold and light.
Each morsel savored, a joy to explore,
A moment of pleasure in every pour.
I linger on sweetness, the spice, the zest,
Grateful for each, my body is blessed.
In this simple act, I find my grace,
Eating with love, fully embraced.

Set Your Intention

Set an intention to be aware of how food affects your body and emotions this week. How will you nourish yourself in a way that supports both physical and emotional health?

Affirmation

"I honor my body by exploring a deeper relationship with food, nourishing myself with love and awareness of how food affects my energy and emotions."

Reflection

✦ How did your relationship with food shift this week?
✦ Did certain foods energize you more than others?

Reflect on any emotional connections you noticed with food, and how this awareness affected your eating habits.

_____

_____

_____

_____

_____

_____

_____

_____

_____

_____

_____

_____

_____

_____

_____

_____

Week 16 : Create a Self-Care Ritual

Nurturing the Growth

Self-care is not just a one-time activity; it's a sacred ritual you can return to again and again. This week, design a self-care ritual that you can perform daily or weekly. Choose activities that bring you peace, joy, and a sense of connection with yourself. It could be a skincare routine, a quiet walk, or a moment of meditation. Whatever it is, make it your own, and make it sacred. Consider:

- What activities make me feel the most cared for and nurtured?
- How can I design a ritual that fits seamlessly into my daily or weekly routine?
- How can I ensure this ritual feels sacred and meaningful?

_____

_____

_____

_____

_____

_____

_____

_____

_____

_____

_____

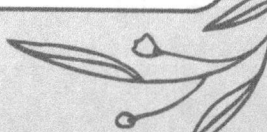

Ritual of Self

I choose me, here and now,
A moment of care, my sacred vow.
With each step, I tend to my heart,
Giving myself the love I've deserved from the start.
In this ritual, I find my peace,
A simple act where worries cease.
This is my time, a choice I make,
To nurture myself for my own sake.

Set Your Intention

At the start of this week, set an intention
to design and practice your self-care ritual.
What will you include to make it sacred
and meaningful to you?

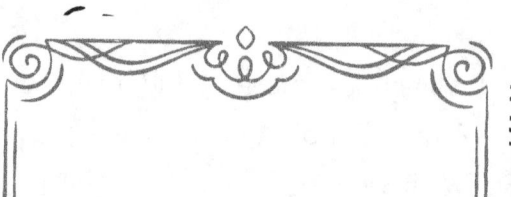

Affirmation

"My self-care ritual is a sacred
act of love toward myself,
providing me with strength,
peace, and joy. In this space, I
am cared for and cherished."

Reflection

 How did creating a self-care ritual impact your week?

Did the ritual help you feel more grounded, connected, and nurtured?

Reflect on any adjustments or insights that made the ritual feel even more meaningful.

Week 17:
Explore Different Types of Movement

Nurturing the Growth

This week, explore different forms of movement that you might not have tried before. From yoga to tai chi, dancing to walking, discover how different movements impact your energy, emotions, and body. Movement is not just about exercise; it's a way to connect with yourself. Try to incorporate a different type of movement each day and observe how it feels. Consider:

- How does movement affect my mood and energy?
- Which types of movement feel most joyful or grounding to me?
- How can I make movement a daily celebration of my body?

_____

_____

_____

_____

_____

_____

_____

_____

_____

_____

_____

The Dance of Self-Love

I move to the beat of my own rhythm,
A slow sway, a gentle stretch,
Each step, a quiet celebration of me.
Breathing in, I find peace,
Breathing out, I release the weight of the day.
In this dance, I'm free—
Moving through my world with grace,
A soft embrace of my body, my space.

Set Your Intention

Set an intention to explore new ways of moving your body this week. How can movement become a celebration of your well-being?

Affirmation

"I honor my body and mind through new forms of movement, embracing the joy and strength it brings. My daily dance of self-love nourishes my whole being."

Reflection

✦ How did trying different types of movement affect your body and mind?

✦ Did you discover a new practice that brought you joy or helped you feel more connected to your body?

Reflect on how you can continue incorporating these movements into your daily routine.

_____

_____

_____

_____

_____

_____

_____

_____

_____

_____

_____

_____

_____

_____

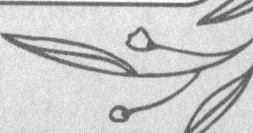

Week 18: Emotional Check-ins

Nurturing the Growth

Take time each day to pause and check in with your emotions. Often, we push through the day without acknowledging how we feel. This week, practice noticing and naming your emotions without judgment. Ask yourself, "How am I feeling right now?" and accept whatever comes up. Consider:

- What emotions are present for me in this moment?
- Am I allowing myself to fully experience my feelings?
- How can I offer compassion to myself when difficult emotions arise?

_____

_____

_____

_____

_____

_____

_____

_____

_____

_____

_____

_____

The Voice of Compassion

I whisper grace in the face of pain,
A tender touch, a soft refrain.
In my heart, the key resides,
To hold myself with love and pride.
No need for blame, no room for shame,
Only kindness where I remain.
In compassion's light, I softly land,
Loving myself, I understand.

Set Your Intention

Set an intention to check in with your emotions throughout the day. How will you offer yourself compassion as you process your feelings?

Affirmation

"I check in with myself regularly, acknowledging and accepting my emotions with kindness and grace."

Reflection

✦ How did taking time to check in with your emotions affect your week?

✦ Did offering yourself compassion help you feel more grounded or supported?

Reflect on how this practice of emotional awareness deepens your self-love journey.

_____

_____

_____

_____

_____

_____

_____

_____

_____

_____

_____

_____

_____

_____

Week 19 : Declutter Your Inner World

Nurturing the Growth

This week, focus on decluttering your mind by releasing limiting beliefs, negative self-talk, and judgments that no longer serve you. Let go of thoughts that keep you stuck and replace them with thoughts that align with your highest good. Consider practicing journaling or meditation to clear out mental clutter. Consider:

- What beliefs or thoughts are holding me back?
- How can I release negative self-talk and embrace thoughts of self-love?
- What new thoughts can I plant to support my growth?

_____

_____

_____

_____

_____

_____

_____

_____

_____

_____

_____

Clarity in Simplicity

Amidst the noise, I crave the still,
Space to breathe, to feel fulfilled.
With each release, I find my way,
In the quiet, I choose to stay.
A sanctuary beyond the rush,
Where peace arrives in every hush.
In simplicity, my soul is free,
Where love and calm come back to me.

Set Your Intention

Set an intention to clear out any limiting
beliefs or negative thoughts this week.
How will you replace them with thoughts
that align with self-love and growth?

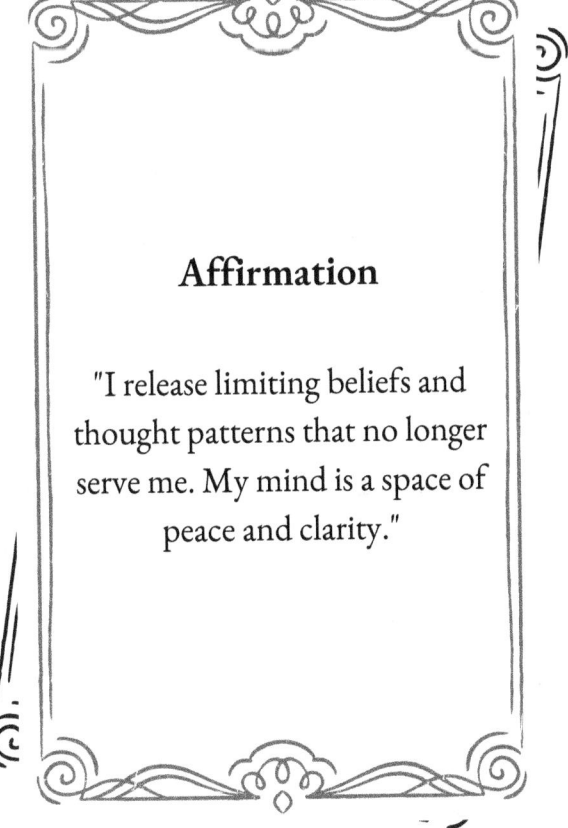

Affirmation

"I release limiting beliefs and
thought patterns that no longer
serve me. My mind is a space of
peace and clarity."

Reflection

✦ How did decluttering your inner world affect your mental state?
✦ Did letting go of negative thoughts help you feel lighter or more at peace?
Reflect on how this mental clarity supports your self-love journey.

_____

_____

_____

_____

_____

_____

_____

_____

_____

_____

_____

_____

_____

_____

_____

_____

Week 20: Try Digital Minimalism

Nurturing the Growth

This week, practice digital minimalism by limiting your screen time and intentionally curating your online content. Pay attention to how much time you spend on your phone or computer, and how different types of media affect your mental and emotional well-being. Choose to engage with content that uplifts and supports you, while letting go of anything that drains your energy or fosters negativity. Consider:

- How much time am I spending on digital devices, and how does it affect me?
- What types of media inspire or uplift me?
- How can I create more intentional digital habits that align with self-love?

_____

_____

_____

_____

_____

_____

_____

_____

_____

Choosing My Views

I sift through the noise,
Picking the melodies that feel right.
Quietly, I reject the chaos—
Choosing only what lifts me higher.
Each word I take in,
Shapes the way I see the world.
So I choose wisely,
With care,
With intention.
In this space, I protect my peace,
And create room for joy.

Set Your Intention

Set an intention to limit your screen time and curate your digital space. How will you create a more mindful relationship with the media you consume?

Affirmation

"I consciously select digital content that enriches my life and aligns with my values. Digital minimalism supports my well-being and presence."

Reflection

 How did practicing digital minimalism affect your mood and mindset this week?

Were there any noticeable benefits to reducing screen time?

Reflect on the impact of creating more mindful digital habits.

_____

_____

_____

_____

_____

_____

_____

_____

_____

_____

_____

_____

_____

_____

Week 21: Connect with Water

Nurturing the Growth

This week, deepen your connection with water, whether it's visiting a natural water source or taking a cleansing bath. Water has the power to cleanse and renew, both physically and emotionally. If you can, spend time by a river, lake, or ocean, allowing the flow of water to calm your spirit. If not, take a salt bath at home or practice mindful hydration by drinking water slowly and with intention. Consider:

- How does water make me feel—calm, refreshed, renewed?
- What emotions or thoughts can I release with the flow of water?
- How can I use water to cleanse and nourish myself this week?

_____

_____

_____

_____

_____

_____

_____

_____

_____

_____

_____

Nature's Embrace

I step outside, breathe in the sky,
Feel the earth beneath, a gentle sigh.
Leaves whisper secrets as I walk,
Nature listens, no need to talk.
With every step, I ground what's true,
Sky wide open, endless blue.
In the oneness, I find my way,
Part of this moment, part of the day.

Set Your Intention

Set an intention to connect with water this week. How will you allow water to cleanse and restore your spirit?

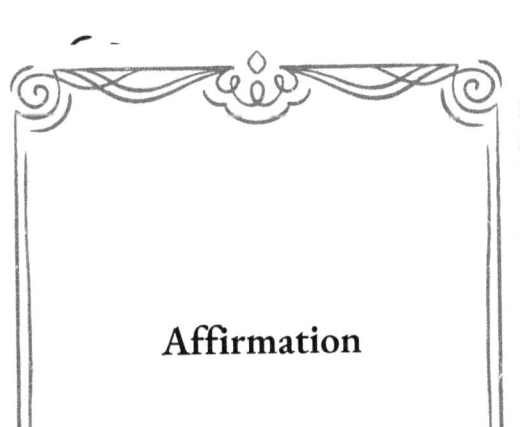

Affirmation

"I connect with water to cleanse, renew, and flow, letting it guide my spirit to peace and balance with ease."

Reflection

✦ How did connecting with water influence your mood or emotional state? Reflect on how water supported your self-love journey this week and what emotions you may have released through this practice.

_____

_____

_____

_____

_____

_____

_____

_____

_____

_____

_____

_____

_____

_____

_____

_____

Week 22:
Develop a Sacred Morning Practice

Nurturing the Growth

A sacred morning practice can anchor you throughout the day, giving you a sense of calm and direction. If you don't already have one, create a morning routine that incorporates multiple elements of self-care—meditation, journaling, breathwork, or gentle movement. If you already have a sacred morning practice, take the time to assess how it's working for you. Add one new element or make adjustments to deepen your experience. Even if you only have 10 minutes, dedicate this time to yourself before the busyness of the day begins. Consider:

- What practices nourish my mind, body, and spirit in the morning?
- How can I create a sacred space or routine that sets the tone for my day?
- What will help me feel grounded and clear as I start the day?

_____

_____

_____

_____

_____

_____

_____

_____

_____

Morning Light

Rise and shine, Divine,
It's time to glow.
As dawn breaks,
Let your energy flow.

A breath, a stretch,
A quiet pause
Filling my spirit,
Just because.

With each moment,
We claim our grace
Morning light,
The sacred space.

Set Your Intention

Set an intention to develop a sacred morning practice. What elements will you include to support your mental, emotional, and spiritual well-being?

Affirmation

"My morning practice nourishes my mind, body, and spirit. Each day begins with clarity and peace."

Reflection

✦ How did creating a sacred morning practice influence your day?
✦ Did you notice a difference in your energy, mood, or clarity?
Reflect on how this morning routine supported your sense of self-love.

_____

_____

_____

_____

_____

_____

_____

_____

_____

_____

_____

_____

_____

_____

_____

_____

_____

Week 23:
Try New Meditation Techniques

Nurturing the Growth

Meditation is a powerful tool for self-love, but not all meditation techniques resonate with everyone. This week, experiment with different styles of meditation, such as loving-kindness meditation, body scan, or breath awareness. Explore what techniques help you feel most centered, peaceful, and connected to yourself. Consider:

- What types of meditation bring me the most peace or clarity?
- How can I explore new techniques to deepen my meditation practice?
- What does meditation feel like when I allow myself to try something new?

_____

_____

_____

_____

_____

_____

_____

_____

_____

_____

Stillness and Flow

I find my breath, in quiet calm,
Releasing the weight, lifting the psalm.
With each inhale, I root within,
With each exhale, a new peace begins.
In this sacred flow, my soul is free,
Where love rises and carries me.
A moment of grace, a deepened space,
In stillness, I find my true pace.

Set Your Intention

Set an intention to explore different meditation techniques this week. How will you create space to try new practices that connect you more deeply to yourself?

Affirmation

"I open myself to different meditation practices to uncover what nurtures my peace and strengthens my connection within."

Reflection

 Which meditation techniques resonated most with you this week?

Did exploring new practices help you feel more connected to yourself? What questions came up for you?

Reflect on how meditation deepened your sense of self-love.

_____

_____

_____

_____

_____

_____

_____

_____

_____

_____

_____

_____

_____

_____

_____

_____

Week 24 : Practice Self-Validation

Nurturing the Growth

This week, focus on self-validation—affirming your worth and accomplishments without seeking approval from others. Practice recognizing and celebrating your own achievements, no matter how small, and remind yourself that you are enough just as you are. Consider:

- What accomplishments or qualities can I validate within myself?
- How can I offer myself praise and recognition without relying on external validation?
- How does self-validation make me feel more empowered?

Affirming My Light

In the quiet of my heart, I see,
The strength and light that's within me.
I need no nod, no outward cheer,
For in my soul, validation's here.
I honor the work that I have done,
In every challenge I have won.
In my own eyes, I stand tall,
Within myself, I have it all.

Set Your Intention

Set an intention to practice self-validation
this week. How will you affirm your own
worth and accomplishments?

Affirmation

"I validate my own worth. I am
enough just as I am, and I
celebrate my unique light."

Week 25 : Time in Silence

Nurturing the Growth

This week, dedicate moments to silence and stillness. Whether it's sitting quietly with your thoughts, taking a silent walk, or spending time in mindful reflection, embrace the power of silence to reconnect with yourself. Silence offers a space to listen to your inner voice and find clarity in the stillness. Consider:

- How does silence help me reconnect with my inner world?
- How can I create more opportunities for quiet moments in my day?
- What clarity can I find when I embrace silence?

_____

_____

_____

_____

_____

_____

_____

_____

_____

_____

_____

_____

The Quiet Within

In the hush, I find my way,
A soft space where worries sway.
No rush, no noise, just me and time,
Here, my peace begins to climb.
With every breath, I slow, I see,
In this quiet, I come to be.
A gentle strength, a voice that's mine,
In silence, I truly shine.

Set Your Intention

Set an intention to embrace silence this week. How can you use moments of silence to find peace and connect with your inner self?

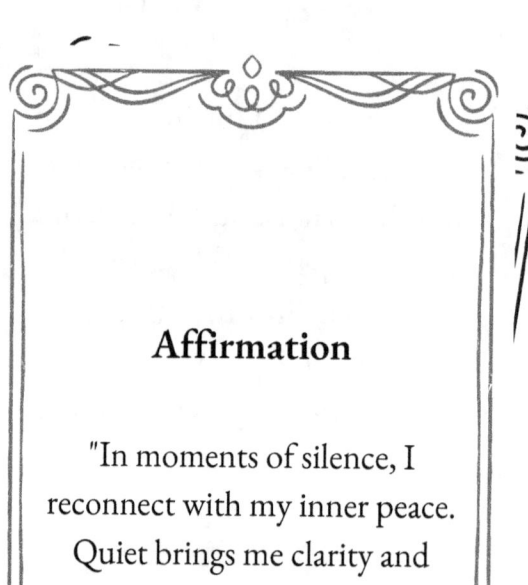

Affirmation

"In moments of silence, I reconnect with my inner peace. Quiet brings me clarity and calm."

Reflection

✦ How did spending time in silence impact your week?
✦ Did you gain any new insights or clarity from your quiet moments?
Reflect on how silence supports your self-love journey and inner growth.

_____

_____

_____

_____

_____

_____

_____

_____

_____

_____

_____

_____

_____

_____

_____

_____

_____

Week 26:
Pause, Reflect, and Set New Goals

Nurturing the Growth

This week, pause and celebrate the progress you've made so far. Reflect on the self-love practices you've incorporated into your life and the growth you've experienced. Once you've celebrated, set clear goals for the next quarter, focusing on how you want to continue nurturing your self-love practices. Consider:

- What accomplishments am I most proud of over the past few weeks?
- How have my self-love practices helped me grow?
- What are my goals for the next quarter, and how can I continue nurturing my growth?

_____

_____

_____

_____

_____

_____

_____

_____

_____

_____

A Celebration of Growth

I pause, reflect, and see with grace,
The journey that's brought me to this place.
Each step, each win, a light that grows,
In the garden of love, where my spirit flows.
I honor the strength that's carried me through,
A path of self-love, ever fresh and new.
I celebrate me, in all I've become,
And with joy, I rise to what's to come.

Set Your Intention

Set an intention to reflect on your progress and celebrate your wins this week. How will you honor your journey while setting goals for your continued growth?

Affirmation

"I honor my journey and celebrate each step forward. With joy, I set new goals for my self-love journey, knowing I am capable of continued growth and transformation."

Reflection

 How did reflecting on your progress make you feel?

Did celebrating your wins and setting new goals inspire you to continue your self-love journey?

Reflect on your accomplishments and how you plan to grow further in the next quarter. Jot your goals down here, as well.

_____

_____

_____

_____

_____

_____

_____

_____

_____

_____

_____

_____

_____

_____

_____

_____

Section 3

Break Free
Overcoming Obstacles to Self-Love

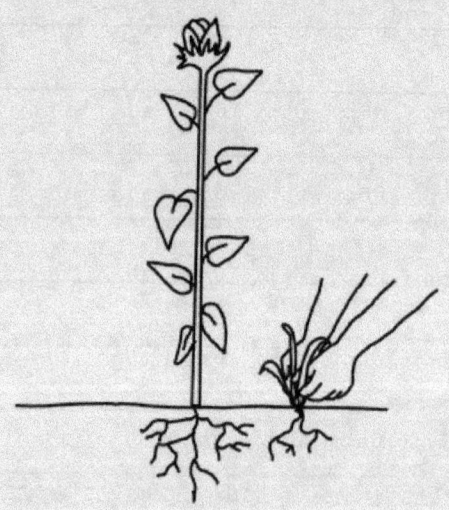

> *"The need for change bulldozed a road down the center of my mind."* – Maya Angelou

Introduction

Maya Angelou's powerful words speak to the heart of transformation—where the need for change becomes undeniable, and we must confront the internal barriers that hold us back. Breaking free from these obstacles isn't easy, but it's necessary for growth. To embody our full power, we must clear away the doubts, fears, and limiting beliefs that choke out our self-love, much like a gardener pulling weeds to allow the flowers to thrive.

In my own journey, I've faced these weeds head-on. There were moments when fear and self-doubt clouded my path, times when I questioned whether I was good enough or worthy of success. I realized that these thoughts were nothing more than obstacles blocking my light, and with time, persistence, and self-compassion, I began the work of pulling them up, one by one. It wasn't always easy, but every weed I removed made more room for love, light, and growth in my life.

In this section, you'll face your own obstacles, from overcoming impostor syndrome to letting go of guilt, and everything in between. It's tough work, but it's powerful work, and each step you take to clear away the weeds will bring you closer to the true, unstoppable version of yourself. As you navigate these weeks, be gentle with yourself—breaking free is a process, and each small step is progress. Together, we'll bulldoze through the obstacles that block your self-love and transform them into stepping stones toward a fuller, more authentic life.

Week 27: Challenge Negative Self-Talk

Uprooting the Weeds

This week, pay close attention to the language you use when speaking to yourself. Negative self-talk can be subtle but has a powerful impact on how you feel about yourself. Start by identifying three common negative phrases you tell yourself, like "I'm not good enough" or "I can't do this." For each negative statement, create a counterstatement that is positive and empowering. Consider:

- What are the recurring negative thoughts I have about myself?
- How can I reframe these thoughts with kindness and compassion?
- How would I speak to a loved one in this situation, and how can I show myself the same love?

_____

_____

_____

_____

_____

_____

_____

_____

_____

_____

Conversations Within

There are voiccs inside me,
whispers I can't ignore.
They cut deep, quietly shaping,
but I am so much more.
Today I choose to listen,
to the words that bring me peace.
To speak to myself with kindness,
and let old judgments cease.

Set Your Intention

Set the intention to become more aware of
your inner dialogue this week. How can
you replace harmful self-talk with words
that uplift and support you?

Affirmation

"I speak to myself with love and
kindness. My words build me
up and illuminate my worth."

Reflection

✦ How did replacing negative self-talk affect your confidence and mood this week?

Reflect on the moments when reframing your thoughts brought you peace or clarity. Notice how changing the way you speak to yourself deepens your self-love.

_____

_____

_____

_____

_____

_____

_____

_____

_____

_____

_____

_____

_____

_____

_____

Week 28: Overcome Impostor Syndrome

Uprooting the Weeds

Impostor syndrome makes us question whether we deserve our achievements, no matter how hard we've worked for them. This week, reflect on times when you've felt like an impostor—when you doubted your abilities or felt like you didn't belong. Write down each instance, and next to it, write a truth about your strengths and accomplishments. Consider:

- When do I feel like an impostor, and why?
- What evidence do I have that proves I am capable and deserving?
- How can I celebrate my successes without minimizing them?

Shadows of Doubt

A shadow follows me,
telling me I don't belong.
But I stand in my own light,
I know this voice is wrong.
For every step I've taken,
I've earned this space I'm in.
No more shrinking back—
it's time for me to win.

Set Your Intention

Set the intention to acknowledge and embrace your achievements this week. How can you replace the feeling of being an impostor with the recognition of your true worth?

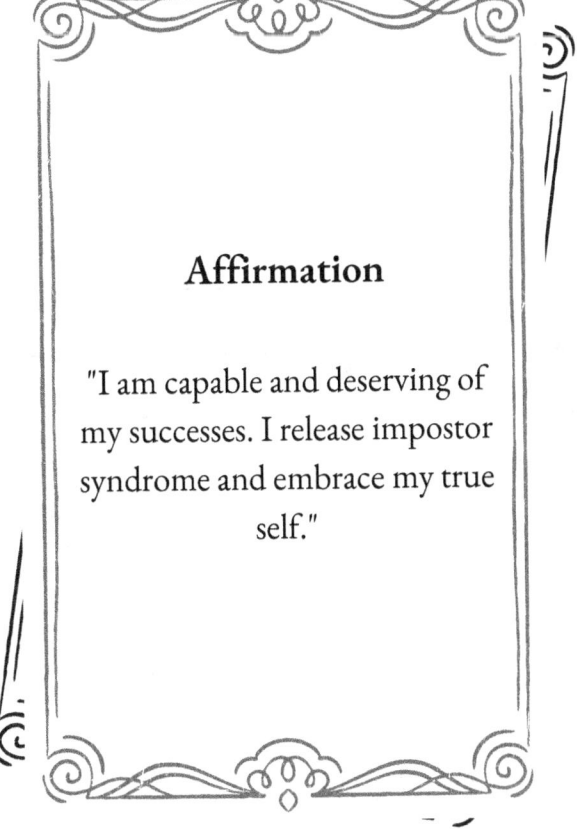

Affirmation

"I am capable and deserving of my successes. I release impostor syndrome and embrace my true self."

Reflection

◆ How did acknowledging your accomplishments shift your perspective?
◆ Did recognizing your strengths make you feel more empowered?
Reflect on how releasing impostor syndrome can deepen your self-love.

_____

_____

_____

_____

_____

_____

_____

_____

_____

_____

_____

_____

_____

_____

_____

_____

_____

_____

Week 29: Release the Fear of Failure

Uprooting the Weeds

Fear of failure often prevents us from taking risks or pursuing our goals. This week, focus on releasing that fear by reframing failure as part of the learning process. Reflect on past situations where the fear of failing held you back, and consider how embracing failure could have helped you grow. Consider:

- What is my biggest fear when it comes to failure, and how does it hold me back?
- How can I view failure as a stepping stone rather than a dead-end?
- What small steps can I take toward a goal, even if failure is possible?

_____

_____

_____

_____

_____

_____

_____

_____

_____

_____

_____

Free from Fear

Failure feels like a wall,
built by my own hands.
Brick by brick, it stands tall,
but now, I understand.
I'll take it down piece by piece,
freeing myself to grow.
In every stumble, there's grace,
a path I'd like to know.

Set Your Intention

Set the intention to embrace failure as a learning opportunity this week. What goal can you pursue with courage, knowing that failure may bring growth and insight?

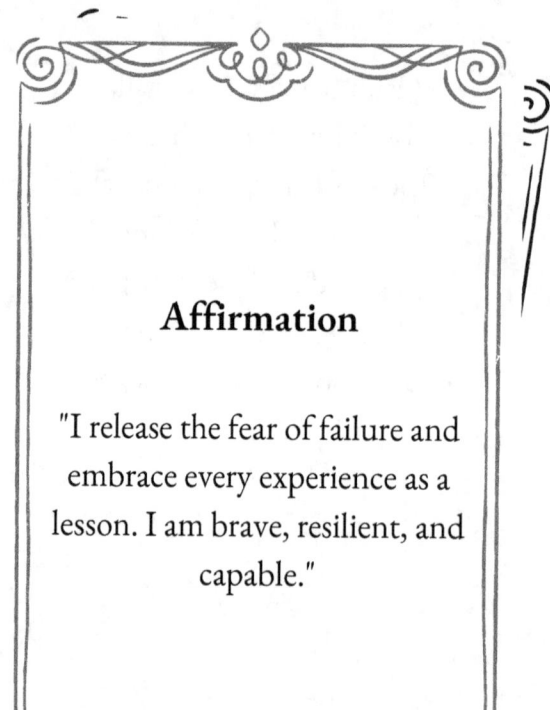

Affirmation

"I release the fear of failure and embrace every experience as a lesson. I am brave, resilient, and capable."

Reflection

- How did confronting your fear of failure impact your actions this week?
- Reflect on what you learned from facing this fear and how it shifted your perception of growth. How has this made space for more self-love and trust in yourself?

_____

_____

_____

_____

_____

_____

_____

_____

_____

_____

_____

_____

_____

_____

_____

Week 30: Break the Comparison Trap

Uprooting the Weeds

Comparison is the thief of joy. This week, commit to breaking the comparison habit. Take a break from social media or limit your time on it, and use that time to engage in activities that nourish your soul. Consider:

- When do I compare myself to others the most, and why?
- How does comparison affect my self-esteem and joy?
- What activities bring me back to myself, reminding me of my uniqueness?

_____

_____

_____

_____

_____

_____

_____

_____

_____

_____

_____

_____

Beyond Comparison's Reach

I've measured myself by others,
their paths seemed so clear.
But today I choose my own,
no longer ruled by fear.
Their success is not my story,
nor a shadow on my own.
In my journey, I find glory,
in the steps I've made alone.

Set Your Intention

Set the intention to limit comparison and focus on your own path this week. How can you celebrate your individuality and stop measuring yourself against others?

Affirmation

"I celebrate my unique journey and release the need to compare myself to others. My path is mine alone, and it is enough."

Reflection

- How did limiting comparison shift your feelings of self-worth?
- Reflect on how focusing on your own path brought a greater sense of peace or contentment. How can you continue this practice to nurture self-love?

_____

_____

_____

_____

_____

_____

_____

_____

_____

_____

_____

_____

_____

_____

_____

_____

Week 31: Handle Rejection Positively

Uprooting the Weeds

Rejection can be painful, but it can also be a redirection toward something better. This week, reflect on a recent rejection and write down what you learned from it. How can you turn that rejection into a lesson or a stepping stone toward growth? Consider:

- How do I typically handle rejection, and why?
- What did this rejection teach me about myself, my needs, or my path?
- How can I use this experience to refocus on my true desires?

_____

_____

_____

_____

_____

_____

_____

_____

_____

_____

_____

_____

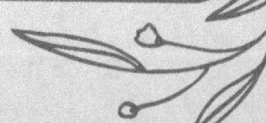

Embracing No

Λ door closes, and I pause,
feeling that echo deep.
But rejection isn't loss,
it's just a chance to leap.
For every "no" I receive,
there's a "yes" waiting near.
The road will shift and lead,
to something bright and clear.

Set Your Intention

Set the intention to see rejection as a redirection this week. How can you shift your mindset from feeling discouraged to feeling empowered by rejection?

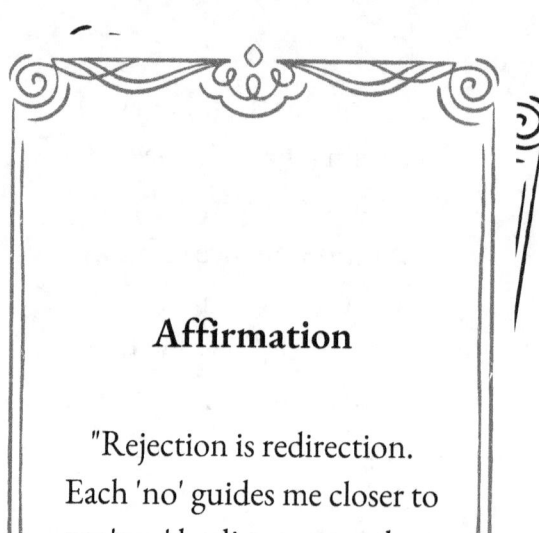

Affirmation

"Rejection is redirection. Each 'no' guides me closer to my 'yes,' leading me to where I'm meant to be."

Reflection

Reflect on how reframing rejection as redirection changed your experience this week.

- Did you feel more empowered?
- How can this new mindset support your self-love journey moving forward?

_____

_____

_____

_____

_____

_____

_____

_____

_____

_____

_____

_____

_____

_____

_____

Week 32: Set Realistic Expectations

Uprooting the Weeds

This week, reflect on the expectations you set for yourself in different areas of your life. Are they too high or unrealistic? Often, we hold ourselves to impossible standards, leading to feelings of inadequacy or burnout. Consider adjusting your expectations to something more achievable, without compromising on your vision for growth. Consider:

- What expectations do I hold for myself, and are they realistic given my current circumstances?
- How do these expectations impact my self-worth and happiness?
- How can I honor my ambition while allowing myself grace?

_____

_____

_____

_____

_____

_____

_____

_____

_____

_____

Balanced Aspirations

I've aimed for distant peaks,
pushed myself too far.
But balance is what I seek,
beneath each guiding star.
I'll honor my ambitions,
without the need to race.
Each step is still a victory,
when taken with grace.

Set Your Intention

Set the intention to find balance in your expectations this week. How can you set goals that honor both your ambition and your current needs?

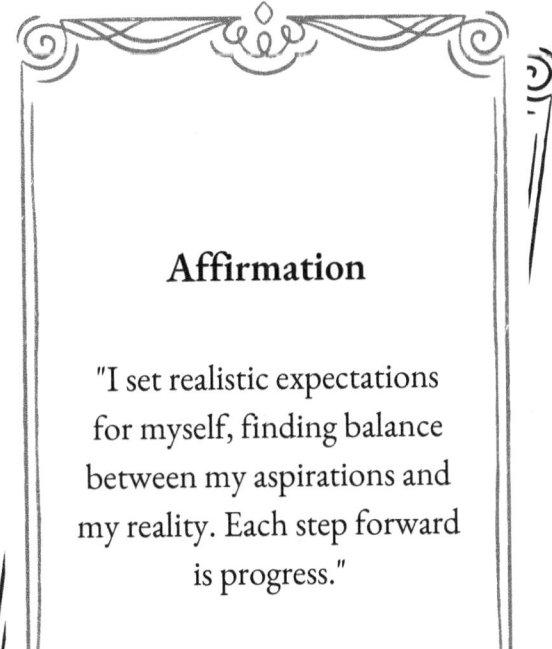

Affirmation

"I set realistic expectations for myself, finding balance between my aspirations and my reality. Each step forward is progress."

Reflection

Take time this week to really observe how adjusting your expectations influences your overall mood and stress levels. Were there moments when lowering your expectations brought more peace or joy? Reflect on how you can continue to practice grace with yourself while still moving toward your goals. Consider how this shift impacts your relationship with self-love:

 Did you notice that letting go of overly ambitious expectations created more space for self-compassion?

 How can you maintain a sense of momentum in your journey while avoiding burnout or discouragement?

_____

_____

_____

_____

_____

_____

_____

_____

_____

_____

_____

_____

_____

_____

Week 33: Foster Resilience

Uprooting the Weeds

Resilience is the ability to bounce back after hardship, but it's also about the strength you gain in the process. This week, reflect on challenges you've faced in the past—whether big or small—and how you overcame them. Create a resilience journal to track your progress and highlight the inner strength that helped you persevere. Consider:

- What were some of the hardest challenges I've faced, and how did I manage to get through them?
- What inner resources (strength, patience, creativity) helped me overcome these challenges?
- How has resilience shaped who I am today?

_____

_____

_____

_____

_____

_____

_____

_____

_____

_____

The Strength to Endure

In the heart of the storm
my strength begins to grow.
It doesn't shout or transform,
but steady, it does show.
Resilience builds in silence,
a calm that holds me still.
In every trial, I find the strength,
to rise again at will.

Set Your Intention

Set the intention to acknowledge your resilience this week. How can you celebrate the strength you've built through adversity?

Affirmation

"I am resilient. With each challenge, I grow stronger and more adaptable, embracing life's lessons with courage."

Reflection

This week, go deeper by considering how resilience has transformed not only your ability to face adversity but your understanding of yourself.

 Reflect on a specific hardship that tested your limits: How did you find strength when you felt depleted?

Were there unexpected moments of grace or insight that came from enduring difficulty?

As you revisit these memories, do you see yourself as more powerful and capable than you originally thought? How can you carry this recognition of resilience forward in your daily life?

_____

_____

_____

_____

_____

_____

_____

_____

_____

_____

_____

_____

Week 34: Embrace Vulnerability

Uprooting the Weeds

Vulnerability often feels like weakness, but in reality, it's one of the most courageous acts of self-love. This week, allow yourself to be vulnerable in a situation where you'd normally hold back. Share a thought, feeling, or aspiration with someone you trust but have been hesitant to express. Consider:

- What areas of my life do I struggle to show vulnerability, and why?
- How can embracing vulnerability lead to deeper connections and more authentic experiences?
- How does fear of rejection or judgment keep me from opening up?

In the Heart's Open Field

Vulnerable, I stand bare,
where I've feared to go.
But in the open air,
I've found a deeper flow.
It's not weakness to reveal,
the truth beneath my skin.
In this rawness, I can heal,
and let the light come in.

Set Your Intention

Set the intention to lean into vulnerability
this week. Where can you soften, share,
and trust more in your interactions with
others?

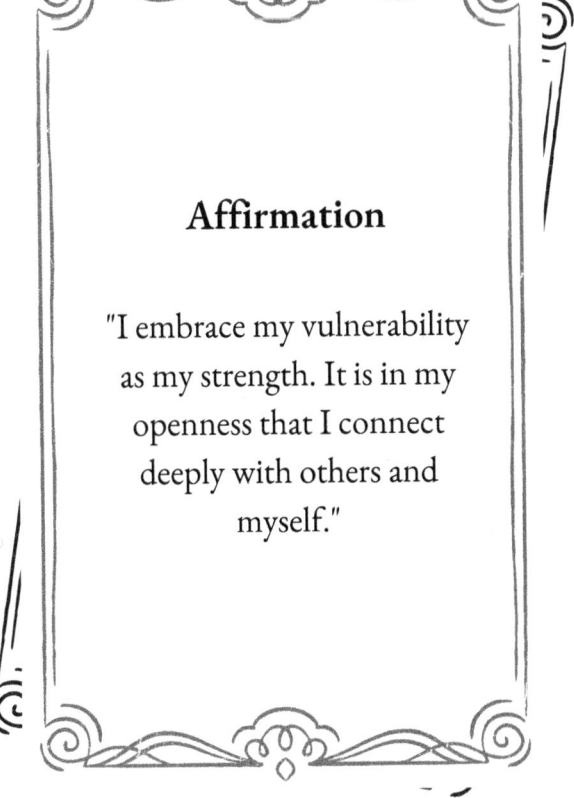

Affirmation

"I embrace my vulnerability
as my strength. It is in my
openness that I connect
deeply with others and
myself."

Reflection

As you move through this week, explore how vulnerability shifted your relationships and your sense of self. Dig deeper into the following questions:

-  How did it feel to let your guard down? Were there moments of discomfort or liberation?
- Did embracing vulnerability lead to more authentic and meaningful connections?

Reflect on how being open allowed you to experience deeper bonds with others or with yourself.

Vulnerability is also about trusting yourself to handle rejection or disappointment—how did facing that fear change your perspective on emotional risk? As you reflect, notice how these moments of openness helped you cultivate self-love and acceptance.

_____

_____

_____

_____

_____

_____

_____

_____

_____

_____

Week 35: Find Strength in Adversity

Uprooting the Weeds

Adversity tests our strength and resilience, but it also offers valuable lessons. This week, reflect on a recent challenge or setback. Write down what you learned from it and how it has made (or can make) you stronger or more resilient. Consider:

- What recent adversity or challenge did I face, and how did it affect me emotionally or mentally?
- How did I respond to this challenge, and what strengths emerged as a result?
- How can I reframe adversity as a powerful tool for growth?

_____

_____

_____

_____

_____

_____

_____

_____

_____

_____

_____

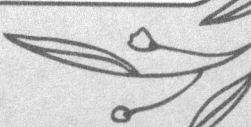

Forged by Fire

Adversity strikes with hcat,
but I don't bend or break.
Instead, I find my feet,
stronger for each quake.
What once felt like a burden,
has shaped me into more.
Now, through every trial,
I'm ready to endure.

Set Your Intention

Set the intention to view adversity as a source of growth this week. How can you approach future challenges with a mindset of strength and resilience?

Affirmation

"I find strength in every adversity. Each challenge I overcome makes me more resilient, wise, and compassionate."

Reflection

Go deeper this week by reflecting on how adversity shaped not only your strength but also your self-perception. Consider these questions:

 How did facing adversity challenge your beliefs about what you're capable of?

 Did this experience reveal inner resources you weren't aware of before? How can you cultivate those resources going forward?

 How has overcoming adversity added to your understanding of self-love?

Reflect on the ways that adversity may have forced you to be kinder to yourself, to dig deeper into your reserves of compassion, or to embrace patience during difficult times.

_____

_____

_____

_____

_____

_____

_____

_____

_____

_____

_____

Week 36: Seek Support When Needed

Uprooting the Weeds

There's a common misconception that seeking support is a sign of weakness. In reality, asking for help requires courage and is a vital part of self-love. This week, reflect on an area of your life where you could use support—whether emotional, physical, or spiritual. Reach out to someone you trust or consider professional help. Consider:

- Why do I hesitate to ask for help? What fears or limiting beliefs hold me back?
- How could receiving support benefit my well-being and growth?
- Who in my life can I turn to for this support?

_____

_____

_____

_____

_____

_____

_____

_____

_____

_____

_____

Together We Rise

We stand stronger, side by side,
in the moments we reach out.
Fortified within ourselves,
yet knowing what support's about.
Together, we rise higher,
than we could on our own.
In unity, we find the strength
to face the unknown.
I lean on you, you lean on me,
and still, we hold our ground.
In this shared space of trust,
our inner strength is found.

Set Your Intention

Set the intention to release the fear of asking for help this week. What steps can you take to trust others with your needs and lean into the support available to you?

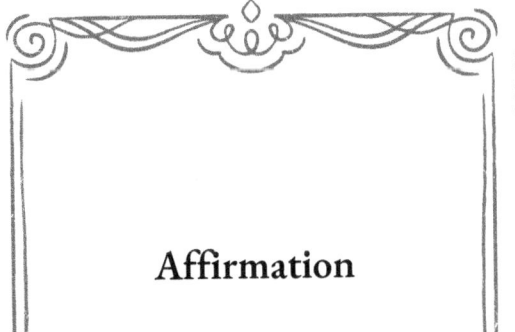

Affirmation

"I am open to seeking and receiving support. It is a sign of strength to ask for help and a step toward nurturing my well-being."

Reflection

As you reflect on your experience of seeking support, go deeper into these questions:

✦ How did it feel to ask for help? Did you experience hesitation, and if so, why?

✦ Did receiving support change your perspective on what it means to be strong? How did it affect your emotional well-being?

Consider the long-term impact of allowing yourself to be supported: How can this practice of openness become a regular part of your self-love routine, allowing you to build stronger relationships and take better care of yourself?

_____

_____

_____

_____

_____

_____

_____

_____

_____

_____

_____

_____

Week 37: Learn from Mistakes

Uprooting the Weeds

Mistakes are inevitable, but they don't define us. This week, reflect on a recent mistake you've made. Instead of dwelling on regret, focus on the lessons this mistake offered. What did it teach you about self-love, personal growth, and resilience? Consider:

- What mistake have I been carrying that I need to release?
- What did this mistake teach me about myself or my needs?
- How can I apply this lesson moving forward, with greater self-compassion and wisdom?

_____

_____

_____

_____

_____

_____

_____

_____

_____

_____

Lessons in the Fall

In my stumble, in my fall,
In my failure, all and all,
Lies a lesson, pure and true,
A step toward a me brand new.
Mistakes are teachers, harsh but fair,
Show me paths to self-care.
In each error, growth I find,
Wisdom gathered, soul refined.

Set Your Intention

Set the intention to embrace mistakes as opportunities for growth this week. How can you shift your mindset from judgment to learning and self-compassion?

Affirmation

"I embrace my mistakes as opportunities for growth, knowing each misstep teaches me valuable lessons about my journey."

Reflection

This week, reflect deeply on the role of mistakes in shaping your self-love journey:

-  Did acknowledging your mistake help release the burden of regret? What emotional or mental freedom came from this release?

- How did recognizing the lessons within your mistake transform your view of failure? Reflect on how learning from mistakes can become a pathway to growth and deeper self-acceptance.

- What specific actions or new behaviors can you take based on the lessons learned, to reinforce a more loving and compassionate approach to yourself?

_____

_____

_____

_____

_____

_____

_____

_____

_____

_____

_____

_____

Week 38: Release Guilt

Uprooting the Weeds

Guilt can be a heavy burden, often tied to past mistakes or decisions. This week, reflect on any lingering guilt that has been weighing on your heart, whether it's related to something recent or from the distant past. Write a letter to yourself in which you forgive yourself for this guilt and release it with kindness. Consider:

- What guilt have I been carrying, and why is it hard to let go?
- How has holding onto this guilt impacted my self-esteem or emotional well-being?
- What would forgiveness look like, and how can I offer myself that grace?

_____

_____

_____

_____

_____

_____

_____

_____

_____

_____

_____

Guilt's Release

There is a weight I've carried,
so familiar it felt like home,
woven into the fabric of my being.
But today, I see it for what it is—
a story long past its conclusion.
I turn the page,
allowing myself the kindness of release,
forgiveness flowing in like breath after too long a pause.
No more chains, no more holding on to what's already gone.
I am lighter now, and in this letting go,
I've found peace.

Set Your Intention

Set the intention to release guilt and practice self-forgiveness this week. How can you approach each day with a lighter heart, free from the weight of the past?

Affirmation

"I release myself from the chains of guilt and embrace forgiveness, understanding that I am deserving of my own compassion and love."

Reflection

Go deeper this week by reflecting on the process of releasing guilt and forgiving yourself:

 How did it feel to finally confront the guilt you've been carrying? Did the process of writing help clarify where the guilt originated and why it persisted?

Did forgiveness come easily, or did you encounter resistance? What part of you still holds on to the need for guilt or punishment, and how can you work through it with compassion?

Reflect on how releasing this guilt has impacted your mental and emotional state. How can you carry this newfound freedom into future decisions and interactions, allowing yourself the grace to move forward?

_____

_____

_____

_____

_____

_____

_____

_____

_____

_____

_____

Week 39: Trust Your Journey

Uprooting the Weeds

Sometimes, self-doubt or impatience makes it difficult to trust that we are on the right path. This week, reflect on your life's journey—past, present, and future. Journal each day about the lessons you've learned and how they have shaped your growth. Take time to appreciate that every step, even the ones that felt uncertain, has brought you closer to your authentic self. Consider:

- How can I trust that I am exactly where I need to be, even if the path looks different than I imagined?
- What moments of growth or change am I most grateful for, and how did those moments shape who I am today?
- What does it look like to trust the unfolding of my journey without rushing or doubting the process?

The Path Within

There is no straight line to becoming.
I have walked through shadows,
stood still in moments of uncertainty,
and pressed on, even when the road disappeared beneath my feet.
Each step, a whisper of trust,
each turn, a lesson waiting to be revealed.
I cannot rush this unfolding—
it is mine to walk, to feel, to know.
And in the quiet between,
I realize:
the journey itself is the destination,
each moment bringing me closer
to the truth that was always mine.

Set Your Intention

Set the intention to trust your unique journey this week. How can you embrace patience and faith, allowing life to unfold in its own time?

Affirmation

"I trust the journey of my life, embracing each phase with grace and faith. I am exactly where I need to be."

Reflection

This week's reflection goes deeper by exploring the lessons learned through trust and surrender:

- Were there moments when trusting your journey felt difficult, and what fears or doubts surfaced during those times? How can you address those fears with compassion?
- Reflect on the times when you tried to rush the process—what did you learn from those moments, and how did they shape your understanding of patience?
- Consider how trusting the journey has expanded your capacity for self-love and acceptance. How has it changed your relationship with time, with your goals, and with the unfolding of your personal growth?

_____

_____

_____

_____

_____

_____

_____

_____

_____

_____

Section 4

Bloom into You
Embracing Your Magical Light

> *"Do not bring people in your life who weigh you down. And trust your instincts... good relationships feel good. They feel right. They don't hurt."* – Michelle Obama

Introduction

As we bloom into the final stage of this journey, it's time to embrace your magical light and cultivate a life rooted in joy, authenticity, and fulfillment. Michelle Obama's words remind us of the power in choosing relationships and experiences that uplift, support, and honor who we truly are. This section is dedicated to helping you release any remaining outside expectations, tap into the core of who you are, and build a life that reflects your deepest values and desires.

By now, you've cultivated a strong foundation of self-love, and many of the practices we've explored should feel like second nature. In this final section, we'll dive deeper into your spiritual wellness, creativity, and the power of community as you align your life with your soul's purpose.

You will also reflect on your growth, rediscover the joy of your inner child, and celebrate the person you've become. This is the time to bloom fully—vibrantly, joyfully, and unapologetically. Your journey has been one of shedding, growing, and blooming. Now, let's continue to nurture the magic within as you step confidently into your light and share it with the world.

Week 40:
Break Free from Outside Expectations

Nurturing the Bloom

This week, focus on releasing the need for outside validation and breaking free from the expectations of others. Reflect on where you have felt confined by societal pressures or others' opinions. Journal about moments when you compromised your truth for acceptance, and explore how you can start making choices aligned with your inner values. Consider:

- How can I release the need for approval from others and trust myself more?
- Where in my life do I still feel trapped by others' expectations, and what steps can I take to break free?
- What does it look like for me to live a life that feels fully aligned with my truth, even when it's different from what others expect?

The Freedom Within

I found freedom where I once felt trapped,
In the space between their words and my truth.
No longer swayed by their expectations,
I walk a path that feels like home.
Their gaze may follow, but it no longer holds me—
I rise, untethered and whole,
Guided by the quiet knowing within,
I am free, and that is enough.

Set Your Intention

This week, set the intention to honor your inner truth and release the need for external validation. How can you create space in your life to nurture your authentic self, free from the weight of outside expectations?

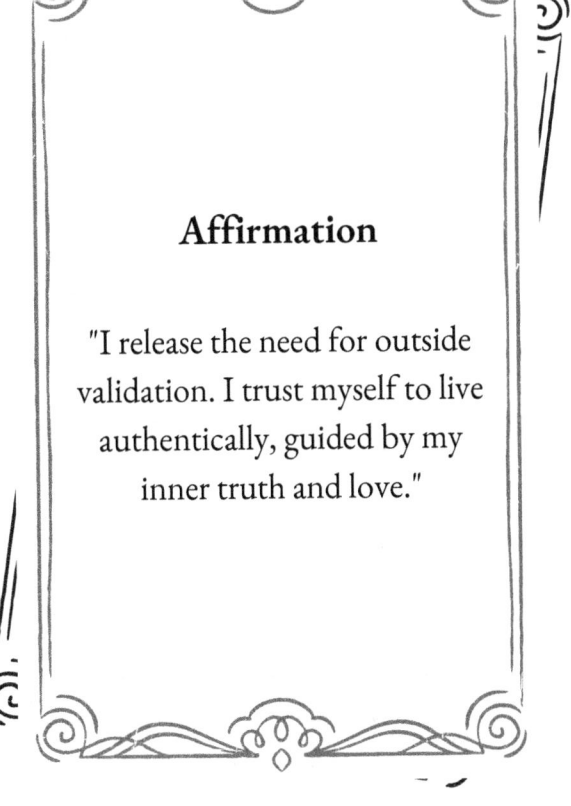

Affirmation

"I release the need for outside validation. I trust myself to live authentically, guided by my inner truth and love."

Reflection

As you reflect on this week, consider these deeper questions to explore how you've embraced your truth:

✦ What areas of your life felt freer this week when you let go of outside expectations?

✦ How did trusting your inner voice affect your choices, and what resistance (if any) came up for you?

Reflect on a time when you felt pressure to conform. How did that experience shape your current understanding of personal freedom, and what lessons did you learn from it?

_____

_____

_____

_____

_____

_____

_____

_____

_____

_____

_____

Week 41:
Surround Yourself with Supportive People

Nurturing the Bloom

This week, focus on the people you allow into your life. Reflect on the relationships that uplift, support, and inspire you, and recognize those that drain your energy. Journal about the positive influence of healthy relationships and how they align with your journey of self-love. Consider:

- Who are the people in my life that bring me the most joy and support?
- How can I cultivate deeper, more meaningful connections with people who encourage my growth?
- Are there relationships that no longer serve me, and how can I create healthy boundaries with these individuals?

_____

_____

_____

_____

_____

_____

_____

_____

_____

_____

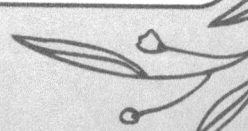

The Circle of Light

In the warmth of their embrace, I grow,
Surrounded by those who let my light show.
Their kindness, a mirror, reflecting back
The love and support that I no longer lack.
Together, we rise, a circle of grace,
In their presence, I find my safe space.
Uplifted, encouraged, with strength renewed
In this circle of light, I am true.

Set Your Intention

This week, set the intention to nurture the relationships that support your highest good. How can you foster a community of love and encouragement around you?

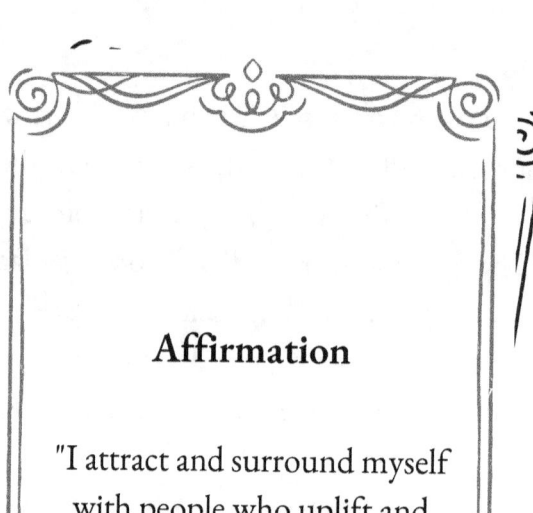

Affirmation

"I attract and surround myself with people who uplift and support me on my journey of self-love and fulfillment."

Reflection

Reflect on your connections this week with the following prompts:

✦ Which relationships brought you the most joy and support, and how did they influence your well-being?

✦ Were there moments when you needed to set boundaries or distance yourself from relationships that drained you?

✦ How can you continue to nurture the relationships that align with your self-love journey, and how has this week impacted your understanding of the power of healthy connections?

_____

_____

_____

_____

_____

_____

_____

_____

_____

_____

_____

_____

_____

Week 42: Rediscover Your Inner Child

Nurturing the Bloom

This week, reconnect with the joy and creativity of your inner child. Take time to engage in activities that bring you pure joy—whether it's coloring, dancing, or simply daydreaming. Reflect on the innocence and playfulness that once came so naturally. Consider:

- What activities did I love as a child that made me feel free and alive?
- How can I bring that sense of wonder and play into my daily life now?
- What part of my inner child still needs to be acknowledged and nurtured?

_____

_____

_____

_____

_____

_____

_____

_____

_____

_____

The Child Within

I find her where laughter lingers,
In the quiet corners of my heart.
She dances in the sunlight,
Chasing dreams, unburdened by time.
Her joy, untouched by expectation,
Reminds me of who I once was
And invites me to be her again,
In the simple beauty of today.

Set Your Intention

This week, set the intention to rediscover
and nurture your inner child. How can
you invite more playfulness and joy into
your life?

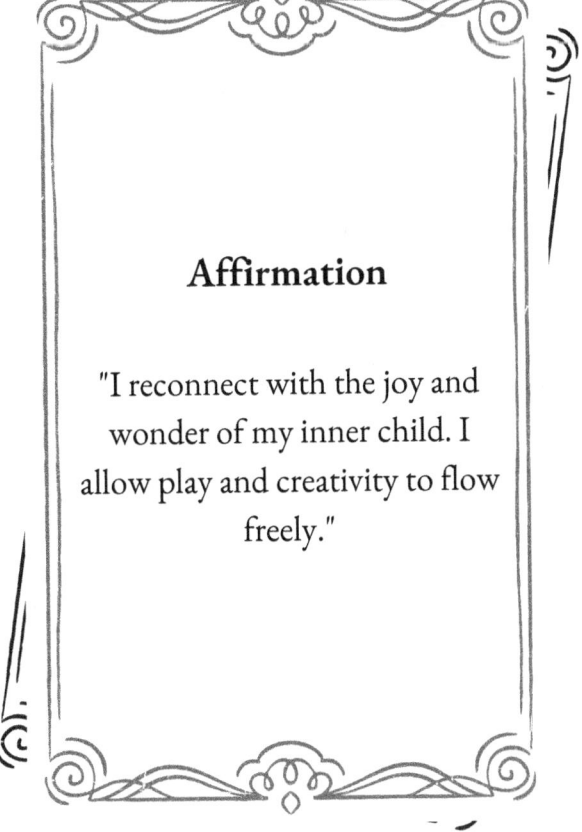

Affirmation

"I reconnect with the joy and
wonder of my inner child. I
allow play and creativity to flow
freely."

Reflection

At the end of the week, reflect on your experiences of reconnecting with your inner child:

✦ What activities brought you the most joy this week, and how did they make you feel?

✦ Were there moments when you hesitated to embrace your inner child? If so, what held you back?

✦ How can you continue to integrate playfulness and creativity into your daily routine, and what did you learn about the importance of joy in your self-love journey?

_____

_____

_____

_____

_____

_____

_____

_____

_____

_____

_____

Week 43:
Engage in Physical Activity for Joy

Nurturing the Bloom

This week, engage in physical activities that bring you joy, rather than focusing on results or perfection. Whether it's dancing, yoga, walking in nature, or any other form of movement that feels freeing, let your body express itself with joy. Consider:

- What types of movement feel most joyful to me, and how can I incorporate them into my week?
- How can I focus on the pleasure of moving my body instead of on performance or outcomes?
- In what ways can physical activity be a celebration of my body's strength, grace, and vitality?

_____

_____

_____

_____

_____

_____

_____

_____

_____

The Joy of Movement

I move, not for the finish line,
But to feel the earth beneath, divine.
Each step, a rhythm, my body sings,
Alive, awake, in what it brings.
No race to win, no goal to chase,
Just freedom, joy, and sacred space.
With every breath, I claim my might,
In motion's flow, I find my light.

Set Your Intention

Set the intention to engage in joyful movement this week. How can you honor your body by moving it with love and celebration, without any attachment to results?

Affirmation

"I embrace physical activity as a source of joy and vitality. My body thrives on movement, and my heart sings with every step."

Reflection

As the week comes to a close, reflect on your experience of joyful movement:

- What types of physical activity brought you the most joy, and how did your body respond?
- Did you feel any pressure to perform or reach a certain standard, and how did you release that?
- How did joyful movement shift your relationship with your body, and how can you continue to celebrate your body's natural rhythms?

_____

_____

_____

_____

_____

_____

_____

_____

_____

_____

_____

_____

_____

_____

Week 44: Incorporate Healthy Eating

Nurturing the Bloom

This week, focus on nourishing your body with healthy, whole foods that make you feel vibrant and alive. Pay close attention to how different foods affect your energy, mood, and overall well-being. Take time to plan meals that honor your body's needs, keeping self-love at the forefront of every choice. Consider:

- How can I approach food with love and gratitude, making choices that nurture my body and soul?
- What foods make me feel energized, vibrant, and alive?
- How can I listen to my body's cues for hunger and fullness, responding with kindness and awareness?

_____

_____

_____

_____

_____

_____

_____

_____

_____

_____

Nourish to Flourish

Each bite, a gift of care,
A moment to honor the body's need.
In the act of nourishing, I remember,
This vessel of mine is worthy of love.
It's not about the rules or restrictions,
But the grace of giving my body what it seeks.
Through food, I flourish,
In nourishment, I bloom.

Set Your Intention

Set the intention to nourish your body with love this week. How can you be mindful of what you consume, treating each meal as an act of self-love?

Affirmation

"I nourish my body with healthy choices, recognizing this as an act of self-love. Each meal brings me closer to vitality and joy."

Reflection

At the end of the week, take a moment to reflect on your experience with nourishing your body:

 How did your relationship with food change when you approached it from a place of love and nourishment?

 Did you notice any shifts in your energy or mood based on the foods you ate?

 How can you continue to make nourishing choices that honor your body's needs while cultivating joy and balance in your life?

_____

_____

_____

_____

_____

_____

_____

_____

_____

_____

_____

_____

_____

Week 45:
Engage in Physical Activity for Joy

Nurturing the Bloom

This week, explore the joy of movement by engaging in physical activities that make you feel alive. Whether it's dancing, yoga, hiking, or simply taking a walk, find moments of movement that connect you to your body in a joyful way. Focus on how movement uplifts your spirit and enhances your sense of vitality. Consider:

- How can I use movement to celebrate my body and the life it supports?
- What activities bring me the most joy and make me feel alive?
- How does movement help me connect to my body in a loving and empowering way?

_____

_____

_____

_____

_____

_____

_____

_____

_____

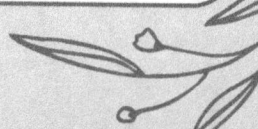

The Joy of Movement

In the stretch of a limb, I feel the pulse of life.
In every step, a celebration.
Not for goals, not for outcomes—
But for the simple joy of being,
Alive and in motion.
Through movement, I find freedom,
A rhythm that reminds me,
I am here, I am whole.

Set Your Intention

Set the intention to move your body with joy this week. How can you use movement as a way to honor and celebrate your life, without focusing on perfection or outcomes?

Affirmation

"I embrace physical activity as a source of joy and vitality. My body thrives on movement, and my heart sings with every step."

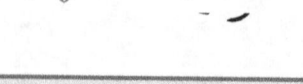

Reflection

Reflect on how joyful movement impacted your physical and emotional well-being this week:

- What forms of movement brought you the most joy, and how did they make you feel in the moment?
- Did you notice any changes in your energy, mood, or outlook as you moved your body with intention and joy?
- How can you continue to embrace movement as a way to connect with your body and celebrate the gift of life?

_____

_____

_____

_____

_____

_____

_____

_____

_____

_____

_____

_____

_____

Week 46: Cultivate Spiritual Wellness

Nurturing the Bloom

This week, focus on practices that nurture your spiritual well-being. Whether it's through meditation, prayer, journaling, or spending time in nature, engage in activities that help you connect with your higher self and the universe. Reflect on the deeper meaning and purpose in your life, and allow yourself to be guided by the inner wisdom that emerges from these practices. Consider:

- What spiritual practices make you feel the most grounded and connected?
- How can you create space in your daily routine for spiritual reflection or connection?
- What insights arise when you quiet your mind and listen to your inner self?

Soul's Serenade

In the quiet moments, a song begins,
Not from the world, but from within.
A gentle call, a soft refrain,
Reminding me that I remain
Connected to something greater—
A light, a love, an endless sky.
In this stillness, I feel the grace,
The spirit's gentle, tender embrace.

Set Your Intention

Set the intention to deepen your spiritual
connection this week. How can you create
more space for practices that nourish your
soul and help you align with your higher self?

Affirmation

"I am committed to my
spiritual wellness, finding peace
and purpose in practices that
connect me to my higher self
and the universe."

Reflection

Reflect on your spiritual wellness and how these practices shaped your sense of inner peace this week:

 What spiritual practices helped you feel most connected and centered?

 How did dedicating time to your spiritual well-being affect your overall outlook and emotional state?

 In what ways can you continue to cultivate spiritual wellness as a foundation for your journey of self-love and growth?

_____

_____

_____

_____

_____

_____

_____

_____

_____

_____

_____

_____

_____

_____

_____

Week 47: Deepen Your Spiritual Practices

Nurturing the Bloom

This week, take your spiritual practices to the next level by exploring deeper forms of connection and reflection. Whether it's meditating for longer periods, connecting with your higher self, or immersing yourself in sacred rituals, aim to strengthen your bond with the divine. Focus on accessing higher wisdom and guidance. Consider:

- How can you deepen your connection to your higher self or the universe this week?
- What advanced spiritual practices can you explore to foster a deeper sense of peace and alignment?
- What truths arise when you commit to spiritual exploration with love and intention?

_____

_____

_____

_____

_____

_____

_____

_____

_____

Spirit's Embrace

In silence, I journey far and deep,
Into spaces where the spirit speaks.
Beyond the noise, beyond the veil,
I find the truth that does not pale.
In this sacred depth, I know,
A boundless love, a gentle glow.
Here I stand, embraced by grace,
My spirit finds its rightful place.

Set Your Intention

Set the intention to deepen your spiritual practice this week. How can you create more intentional time for spiritual reflection and connection, allowing your spirit to flourish?

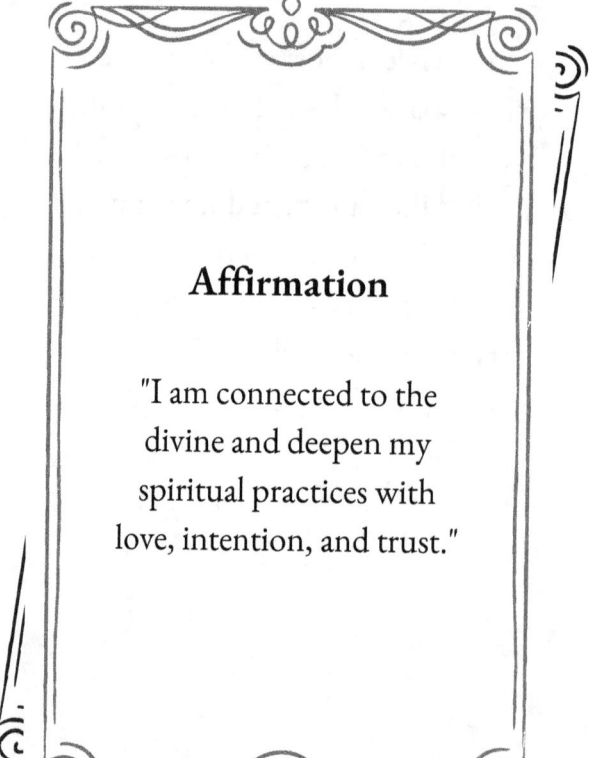

Affirmation

"I am connected to the divine and deepen my spiritual practices with love, intention, and trust."

Reflection

Reflect on the spiritual practices you deepened this week and the insights they brought:

- What new spiritual practices or deeper forms of existing ones helped you feel most aligned?
- How did these advanced practices affect your sense of inner peace and connection with your higher self?
- How can you continue nurturing your spiritual growth and deepen your connection with the divine going forward?

_____

_____

_____

_____

_____

_____

_____

_____

_____

_____

_____

_____

_____

Week 48: Engage in Community Service

Nurturing the Bloom

This week, step outside yourself and into your community. Identify a way to give back, whether through volunteering, offering help to a neighbor, or participating in an act of kindness. Reflect on how serving others nurtures your sense of connection and enriches your own life. Consider:

- How can you serve your community in a way that feels meaningful to both you and those around you?
- What skills or gifts do you have that could benefit others?
- How does giving back reinforce your self-love and your sense of purpose?

_____

_____

_____

_____

_____

_____

_____

_____

_____

_____

_____

Hands United

In the joining of hands, we rise,
Strength found in the light of others' eyes.
A shared burden, a shared heart,
In this service, we each play our part.
Through giving, I see love grow,
In helping, I feel the flow.
Together we rise, together we stand,
In service, I lend a hand.

Set Your Intention

Set the intention to engage in community service this week. How can you approach this with a heart full of love, knowing that giving to others nurtures both yourself and them?

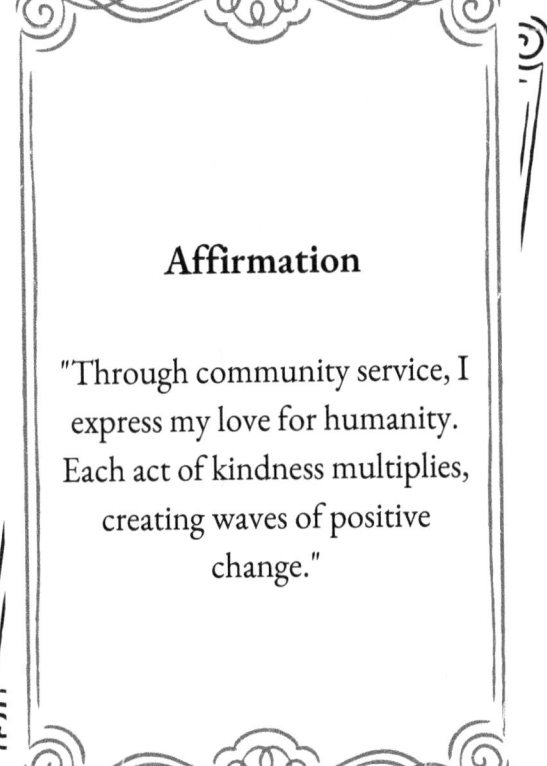

Affirmation

"Through community service, I express my love for humanity. Each act of kindness multiplies, creating waves of positive change."

Reflection

Reflect on your experiences with community service this week:

 How did the act of giving make you feel? Did you notice any changes in your mood, energy, or perspective?

 How did your service foster a deeper sense of connection with your community?

 What did you learn about yourself through serving others, and how does this contribute to your self-love journey?

Week 49:
Align Your Life with Your Soul's Purpose

Nurturing the Bloom

This week, reflect on the alignment between your life and your soul's purpose. Consider the direction you are heading in and whether it aligns with your deepest values, desires, and unique gifts. Take some time to journal about what truly fulfills you and how you can integrate more of that into your life. Consider:

- What are the passions or talents that light you up? How can you pursue them more actively?
- How aligned are your current daily activities with your soul's purpose?
- What small changes can you make to ensure that you are living in alignment with your truest self?

_____

_____

_____

_____

_____

_____

_____

_____

The Path Ahead

I walk not in someone else's shoes
but on a road only I can choose.
The map is within, not drawn by another,
and the compass, my heart, the guide I uncover.
Each step I take is a return to me,
aligned with the truth I am meant to be.

Set Your Intention

Set the intention to align your actions, thoughts, and decisions with your soul's purpose this week. What small steps can you take to live more authentically in your truth?

Affirmation

"I align my life with my passion and soul's purpose, creating a reality that fulfills me on every level."

Reflection

Reflect on your alignment with your soul's purpose:

- What actions did you take this week to align your life with your soul's desires?
- How did these changes or reflections impact your sense of fulfillment and joy?
- What further steps can you take to live more fully in alignment with your soul's purpose?

_____

_____

_____

_____

_____

_____

_____

_____

_____

_____

_____

_____

_____

_____

Week 50: Plan for a Future with Self-Love

Nurturing the Bloom

This week, shift your focus toward the future. Think about the life you wish to create—one rooted in self-love, joy, and authenticity. Write down your goals and intentions for the coming year, focusing on how you will continue to nurture your growth. Consider:

- What does your ideal future look like when self-love is at its core?
- How can you continue the practices you've cultivated throughout this journey?
- What steps will you take to stay true to yourself as you move forward?

_____

_____

_____

_____

_____

_____

_____

_____

_____

_____

_____

_____

Horizon of Self-Love

The road ahead is wide and bright,
lit by the love I've cultivated, light by light.
Each goal, a reflection of the truth I hold,
each step, a journey into something bold.
I move forward, steady and free,
with love as my guide, my future is me.

Set Your Intention

Set the intention to plan your future with love and care, knowing that your path is guided by self-compassion and personal growth.

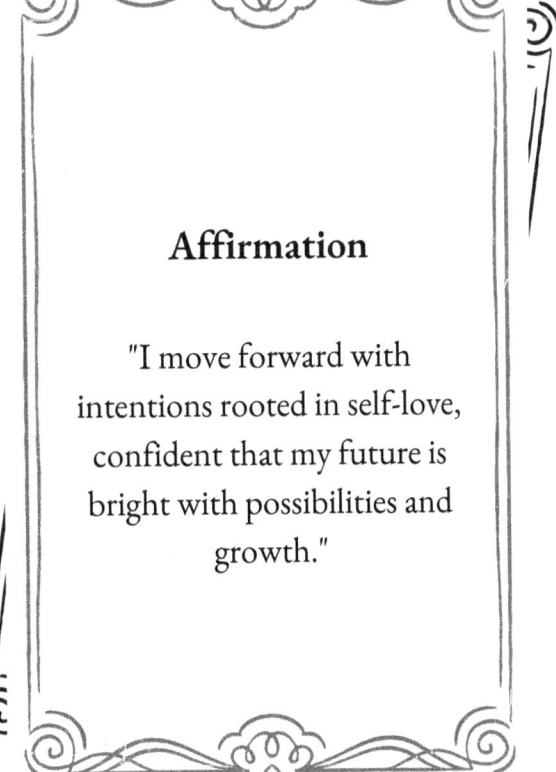

Affirmation

"I move forward with intentions rooted in self-love, confident that my future is bright with possibilities and growth."

Reflection

Reflect on your plans for the future:
- How does self-love shape the vision you have for your future?
- What are the core values and practices you will continue to honor as you move forward?
- How do these intentions reflect the growth and lessons you've learned on this journey?

_____

_____

_____

_____

_____

_____

_____

_____

_____

_____

_____

_____

_____

_____

Week 51:
Create a Vision Board for the Future

Nurturing the Bloom

This week, dedicate time to creating a vision board that represents your future self—one who is fully aligned with self-love and purpose. Use images, words, and symbols that reflect your goals, desires, and the energy you wish to carry forward. Consider:

- What does your most fulfilled, joyful, and authentic self look like?
- What do you want to manifest in the coming months or years?
- How can your vision board serve as a reminder of your journey and your growth?

_____

_____

_____

_____

_____

_____

_____

_____

_____

The Bloom Ahead

The future stretches out before me,
a canvas waiting for the colors I choose.
With every dream, every hope,
I paint a life that feels true to my soul.
In the quiet of intention,
I create the path that's meant to be.

Set Your Intention

Set the intention to create a vision that
aligns with your highest self and future
goals. How can this vision board inspire
you to stay rooted in self-love as you
continue to bloom?

Affirmation

"My vision board reflects the
dreams and desires of my true
self, guiding me toward a future
filled with love, purpose, and
joy."

Reflection

Reflect on your vision board:

✦ How did the process of creating your vision board feel?

✦ What feelings or emotions came up as you visualized your future?

✦ How will you use this vision board as a tool to stay aligned with your self-love journey moving forward?

_____

_____

_____

_____

_____

_____

_____

_____

_____

_____

_____

_____

Week 52:
Reflect and Celebrate Your Growth

Nurturing the Bloom

This final week is dedicated to reflection and celebration. Take time to look back at your journey and honor the growth, lessons, and breakthroughs you've experienced. Celebrate how far you've come and the strength you've cultivated. Consider:

- How has your relationship with yourself evolved over these 52 weeks?
- What are the most significant lessons you've learned along the way?
- How can you honor yourself and this journey as you move forward?

_____

_____

_____

_____

_____

_____

_____

_____

_____

_____

The Garden Grows

I look back at the seeds I planted,
tended with care, love, and time.
Now, I see the garden in full bloom—
each flower a symbol of the growth I've claimed.
I celebrate not just the outcome,
but the journey that made me whole.

Set Your Intention

Set the intention to celebrate your growth
and honor the work you've done. What
small or large acts of self-celebration can
you engage in this week to mark the end of
this transformative journey?

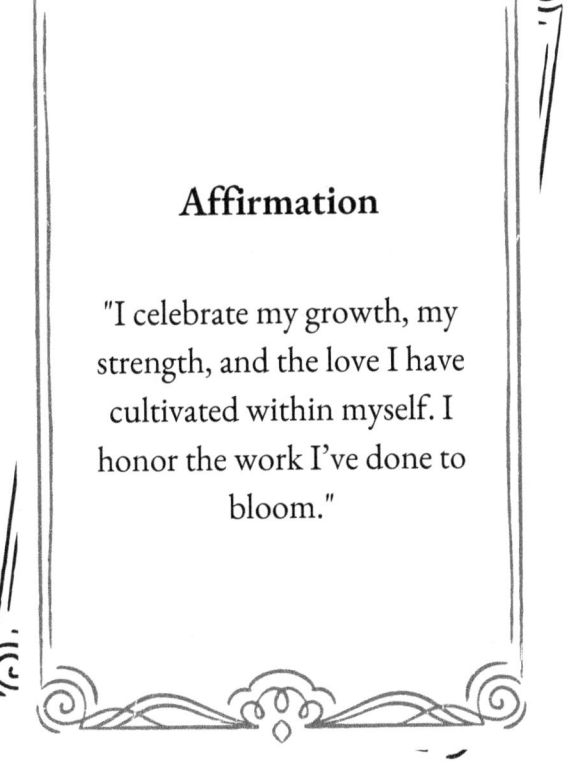

Affirmation

"I celebrate my growth, my
strength, and the love I have
cultivated within myself. I
honor the work I've done to
bloom."

Reflection

Reflect on your journey:

 What moments or milestones stand out most as pivotal on your path to self-love?

How can you continue to nurture the growth you've achieved?

How will you carry the lessons from these 52 weeks into the future, ensuring self-love remains at the center of your life?

_____

_____

_____

_____

_____

_____

_____

_____

_____

_____

_____

_____

_____

_____

Conclusion

The Journey Continues
Stepping Fully into Your Magic

As our season together in *Bloom in Any Season: 52 Ways to Grow into Your Magical Self* gently winds down, take a moment to reflect on the beautiful transformation you've undergone. Each week, each practice, each poem has been a petal contributing to the radiant bloom you are today. Through actions, affirmations, and moments of self-discovery, you've nurtured the soil of self-appreciation, weathered the storms of self-doubt, and basked in the sunlight of joy, love, and fulfillment.

But this is not the end of your journey—it's a new beginning. The essence of self-love you've cultivated here isn't meant to be confined to these pages. It is a living, breathing energy that will continue to grow, evolve, and thrive with your ongoing care. This journey isa continuous cycle of blooming, shedding, and blooming again. Self-love is the water that sustains your growth, the sunlight that illuminates your path, and the rich soil that anchors you as you explore your limitless potential.

As you step into the next chapter of your life, let the lessons from these weeks guide you. These insights are now a part of you—woven into the fabric of your being, always ready to be called upon in moments of need or celebration. Let them remind you of the resilience you've discovered, the joy you've uncovered, and the magic you've reclaimed. You are not just surviving; you are thriving. You are not just existing; you are blossoming in every season.

Your **Gardener's Log** is a faithful record of your growth to support you in continuing this journey. Every entry, every reflection is a leaf unfurled, a root strengthened—a tangible reminder of how far you've come. This log is your companion, a testament to the nurturing you've provided yourself, and a guide for future growth.

When you seek further nourishment, turn to the **Resources to Grow & Maintain**. From inspiring books and podcasts to soothing music, these carefully curated resources are here to keep your self-love garden flourishing. Each recommendation is a tool to help you deepen your practice and sustain the bloom of self-love that you've worked so hard to cultivate.

The journey of self-love is one of constant renewal. It requires patience, kindness, and the willingness to embrace each new phase with an open heart. Just as the seasons change, so will you—forever growing, evolving, and stepping deeper into your magic.

As you continue, carry with you the wisdom of the petals and leaves you've gathered. May you always find strength in your vulnerability, beauty in your authenticity, and an endless well of love within. Your journey is unique, and your bloom is a reflection of your soul's light—vivid, powerful, and infinitely worthy.

Parting Activation

"I step into each day with the grace of a blooming flower, embracing my journey of self-love as the masterpiece of my heart. With every breath, I promise to nourish, cherish, and honor myself. I am a vessel for the universe's boundless love, and I receive it with open arms and an open heart."

Let this book remain a cherished companion along your path—a testament to your worth, your growth, and the greatest love of all: the love that blooms within you.

"May your spirit be light and your soul be free."
- Dr. Makeba Morgan Hill

Gardener's Log:
Quick Reference Guide to Growth

This Gardener's Log is your personal record of growth, reflection, and blossoming throughout your self-love journey. It invites you to recognize the nurturing you've given yourself, the storms you've weathered, and the joy you've cultivated along the way. Each entry celebrates your resilience, your willingness to evolve, and your unfolding journey toward full bloom.

For ease of reference, all affirmations and poems from each week are indexed here, allowing you to quickly revisit the words or poetic reflections that resonated with you most. Every mark you make in this log is a leaf unfurled, a flower blossomed, and a root deepened—each one a vital step in your ongoing journey toward flourishing in self-love.

This log is a testament to the care, love, and attention you've invested in yourself and serves as a guiding light as you continue to nurture your growth garden.

Section 1: Awaken the Magic Within: Discovering Self-Love

Planting the Seeds – In this phase, we laid the foundation for growth by discovering and nourishing the roots of self-love. With each action, you planted the seeds that will bloom into a more vibrant, authentic version of yourself.

☐ **Week 1: Identify Your Values**
- <u>Poem:</u> The Core of Me
- <u>Affirmation:</u> "I am grounded in my values, which guide me in every decision. Each choice brings me closer to my true self."

☐ **Week 2: Set Healthy Boundaries**
- <u>Poem:</u> Boundaries: My Sacred Space
- <u>Affirmation:</u> "I honor my limits and assert my needs with clarity and strength. My boundaries protect my peace and well-being."

☐ **Week 3: Cultivate Gratitude**
- <u>Poem:</u> Gratitude's Gentle Embrace
- <u>Affirmation:</u> "Each day, I find new reasons to be grateful. My heart overflows with appreciation for the abundance in my life."

☐ **Week 4: Explore Your Creativity**
- <u>Poem:</u> The Dance of Creativity
- <u>Affirmation:</u> "Creativity flows through me effortlessly. I embrace my artistic expressions with an open heart and mind."

☐ **Week 5: Prioritize Your Health**
- <u>Poem:</u> A Vow to My Body
- <u>Affirmation:</u> "I honor my body with choices that promote health and vitality. My commitment to my well-being is an act of self-love."

☐ **Week 6: Practice Mindfulness**
- <u>Poem:</u> In This Moment
- <u>Affirmation:</u> "With each breath, I anchor myself in the present moment. I embrace mindfulness as a way to feel calm and centered."

☐ **Week 7: Deepen Your Sleep Ritual**
- <u>Poem:</u> The Night's Embrace
- <u>Affirmation:</u> "I honor my need for restful sleep. My nightly rituals nurture my body and soul, helping me wake up refreshed."

- [ ] **Week 8: Connect with Nature**
  - o <u>Poem</u>: Nature's Caress
  - o <u>Affirmation</u>: "I find harmony and peace in nature's embrace. Connecting with the earth grounds me and fills my soul with joy."
- [ ] **Week 9: Foster New Connections**
  - o <u>Poem</u>: Bridges Between Hearts
  - o <u>Affirmation</u>: "I open my heart to meaningful connections, knowing each person I meet reflects a part of me. Building bridges enriches my life and nourishes my soul."
- [ ] **Week 10: Practice Self-Compassion**
  - o <u>Poem</u>: The Voice of Compassion
  - o <u>Affirmation</u>: "I treat myself with kindness and compassion. I offer myself grace and understanding as I navigate life's challenges."
- [ ] **Week 11: Practice Forgiveness**
  - o <u>Poem</u>: The Path to Forgiveness
  - o <u>Affirmation</u>: "I choose forgiveness, freeing myself and others from the past. In forgiveness, I find peace and the strength to heal and move forward."
- [ ] **Week 12: Pause for Self-Reflection**
  - o <u>Poem</u>: The Mirror Within
  - o <u>Affirmation</u>: "I pause for self-reflection, honoring the growth and wisdom I uncover within. Each moment of introspection brings me closer to my true self."
- [ ] **Week 13: Take Time to Celebrate Wins**
  - o <u>Poem</u>: A Celebration of Me
  - o <u>Affirmation</u>: "I honor my progress and celebrate my wins, no matter how big or small. Each step forward is a testament to my growth."

Section 2: Living in Your Light: Practicing Self-Love Daily

Nurturing the Seedlings – With the foundation laid, we have also nurtured the seedlings of self-love. Daily practices support steady growth, strengthening your ability to live in alignment with your values and embrace your light.

- ☐ **Week 14: Begin Your Day with Intention**
  - Poem: Dawn's Promise
  - Affirmation: "Each morning, I set my intention, guiding my actions and thoughts throughout the day. My intention shapes my reality and aligns with my inner truth."

- ☐ **Week 15: Deepen Your Relationship with Food**
  - Poem: A Meal, A Moment
  - Affirmation: "I honor my body by exploring a deeper relationship with food, nourishing myself with love and awareness of how food affects my energy and emotions."

- ☐ **Week 16: Create a Self-Care Ritual**
  - Poem: Ritual of Self
  - Affirmation: "My self-care ritual is a sacred act of love toward myself, providing me with strength, peace, and joy. In this space, I am cared for and cherished."

- ☐ **Week 17: Explore Different Types of Movement**
  - Poem: The Dance of Self-Love
  - Affirmation: "I honor my body and mind through new forms of movement, embracing the joy and strength it brings. My daily dance of self-love nourishes my whole being."

- ☐ **Week 18: Emotional Check-ins**
  - Poem: The Voice of Compassion
  - Affirmation: "I check in with myself regularly, acknowledging and accepting my emotions with kindness and grace."

- ☐ **Week 19: Declutter Your Inner World**
  - Poem: Clarity in Simplicity
  - Affirmation: "I release limiting beliefs and thought patterns that no longer serve me. My mind is a space of peace and clarity."

- ☐ **Week 20: Try Digital Minimalism**
  - ○ <u>Poem:</u> Choosing My Views
  - ○ <u>Affirmation:</u> "I consciously select digital content that enriches my life and aligns with my values. Digital minimalism supports my well-being and presence."
- ☐ **Week 21: Connect with Water**
  - ○ <u>Poem:</u> Nature's Embrace
  - ○ <u>Affirmation:</u> "I connect with water to cleanse and renew my spirit, deepening my bond with the natural world."
- ☐ **Week 22: Develop a Sacred Morning Practice**
  - ○ <u>Poem:</u> Morning Light
  - ○ <u>Affirmation:</u> "My morning practice nourishes my mind, body, and spirit. Each day begins with clarity and peace."
- ☐ **Week 23: Try New Meditation Techniques**
  - ○ <u>Poem:</u> Stillness and Flow
  - ○ <u>Affirmation:</u> "I open myself to different meditation practices to uncover what nurtures my peace and strengthens my connection within."
- ☐ **Week 24: Practice Self-Validation**
  - ○ <u>Poem:</u> Affirming My Light
  - ○ <u>Affirmation:</u> "I validate my own worth. I am enough just as I am, and I celebrate my unique light."
- ☐ **Week 25: Time in Silence**
  - ○ <u>Poem:</u> The Quiet Within
  - ○ <u>Affirmation:</u> "In moments of silence, I reconnect with my inner peace. Stillness brings me clarity and calm."
- ☐ **Week 26: Pause, Reflect, and Set New Goals**
  - ○ <u>Poem:</u> A Celebration of Growth
  - ○ <u>Affirmation:</u> "I honor my journey and celebrate each step forward. With joy, I set new goals for my self-love journey, knowing I am capable of continued growth and transformation."

Section 3: Breaking Free: Overcoming Obstacles to Self-Love

Uprooting the Weeds – As you have been bloom, challenges have arisen that threaten to choke your growth. In this phase, we focused on removing limiting beliefs, fears, and external expectations, allowing your self-love to flourish freely.

- ☐ **Week 27: Challenge Negative Self-Talk**
  - ○ <u>Poem:</u> Conversations Within
  - ○ <u>Affirmation:</u> "I speak to myself with love and kindness. My words build me up and illuminate my worth."
- ☐ **Week 28: Overcome Impostor Syndrome**
  - ○ <u>Poem:</u> Shadows of Doubt
  - ○ <u>Affirmation:</u> "I am capable and deserving of my successes. I release impostor syndrome and embrace my true self."
- ☐ **Week 29: Release the Fear of Failure**
  - ○ <u>Poem:</u> Free from Fear
  - ○ <u>Affirmation:</u> "I release the fear of failure and embrace every experience as a lesson. I am brave, resilient, and capable."
- ☐ **Week 30: Break the Comparison Trap**
  - ○ <u>Poem:</u> Beyond Comparison's Reach
  - ○ <u>Affirmation:</u> "I celebrate my unique journey and release the need to compare myself to others. My path is mine alone, and it is enough."
- ☐ **Week 31: Handle Rejection Positively**
  - ○ <u>Poem:</u> Embracing No
  - ○ <u>Affirmation:</u> "Rejection is redirection. Each 'no' guides me closer to my 'yes,' leading me to where I'm meant to be."
- ☐ **Week 32: Set Realistic Expectations**
  - ○ <u>Poem:</u> Balanced Aspirations
  - ○ <u>Affirmation:</u> "I set realistic expectations for myself, finding balance between my aspirations and my reality. Each step forward is progress."
- ☐ **Week 33: Foster Resilience**
  - ○ <u>Poem:</u> The Strength to Endure
  - ○ <u>Affirmation:</u> "I am resilient. With each challenge, I grow stronger and more adaptable, embracing life's lessons with courage."

- [ ] **Week 34: Embrace Vulnerability**
  - Poem: In the Heart's Open Field
  - Affirmation: "I embrace my vulnerability as my strength. It is in my openness that I connect deeply with others and myself."
- [ ] **Week 35: Find Strength in Adversity**
  - Poem: Forged by Fire
  - Affirmation: "I find strength in every adversity. Each challenge I overcome makes me more resilient, wise, and compassionate."
- [ ] **Week 36: Seek Support When Needed**
  - Poem: Together We Rise
  - Affirmation: "I am open to seeking and receiving support. It is a sign of strength to ask for help and a step toward nurturing my well-being."
- [ ] **Week 37: Learn from Mistakes**
  - Poem: Lessons in the Fall
  - Affirmation: "I embrace my mistakes as opportunities for growth, knowing each misstep teaches me valuable lessons about my journey."
- [ ] **Week 38: Release Guilt**
  - Poem: Guilt's Release
  - Affirmation: "I release myself from the chains of guilt and embrace forgiveness, understanding that I am deserving of my own compassion and love."
- [ ] **Week 39: Trust Your Journey**
  - Poem: The Path Within
  - Affirmation: "I trust the journey of my life, embracing each phase with grace and faith. I am exactly where I need to be."

Section 4: Bloom into You: Embracing Your Magical Light

Nurturing the Bloom—In this phase, you're nurturing your true self. The seeds of self-love have blossomed. It's time to fully embrace and support your growth, live in alignment with your soul's purpose and radiate your unique magic.

- ☐ **Week 40: Break Free from Outside Expectations**
  - ○ <u>Poem:</u> The Freedom Within
  - ○ <u>Affirmation:</u> "I release the need for outside validation. I trust myself to live authentically, guided by my inner truth and love."
- ☐ **Week 41: Surround Yourself with Supportive People**
  - ○ <u>Poem:</u> The Circle of Light
  - ○ <u>Affirmation:</u> "I attract and surround myself with people who uplift and support me on my journey of self-love and fulfillment."
- ☐ **Week 42: Rediscover Your Inner Child**
  - ○ <u>Poem:</u> The Child Within
  - ○ <u>Affirmation:</u> "I reconnect with the joy and wonder of my inner child, allowing play and creativity to flow freely."
- ☐ **Week 43: Engage in Physical Activity for Joy**
  - ○ <u>Poem:</u> The Joy of Movement
  - ○ <u>Affirmation:</u> "I embrace physical activity as a source of joy and vitality. My body thrives on movement, and my heart sings with every step."
- ☐ **Week 44: Incorporate Healthy Eating**
  - ○ <u>Poem:</u> Nourish to Flourish
  - ○ <u>Affirmation:</u> "I nourish my body with healthy choices, recognizing this as an act of self-love. Each meal brings me closer to vitality and joy."
- ☐ **Week 45: Explore Creative Outlets**
  - ○ <u>Poem:</u> Creativity's Flow
  - ○ <u>Affirmation:</u> "My creativity is a gateway to my inner self and a source of joy. Through artistic expression, I connect deeply with my true essence."

- ☐ **Week 46: Cultivate Spiritual Wellness**
  - ○ Poem: Soul's Serenade
  - ○ Affirmation: "I am committed to my spiritual wellness, finding peace and purpose in practices that connect me to my higher self and the universe."
- ☐ **Week 47: Deepen Your Spiritual Practices**
  - ○ Poem: Spirit's Embrace
  - ○ Affirmation: "I am connected to the divine and deepen my spiritual practices with love, intention, and trust."
- ☐ **Week 48: Engage in Community Service**
  - ○ Poem: Hands United
  - ○ Affirmation: "Through community service, I express my love for humanity. Each act of kindness multiplies, creating waves of positive change."
- ☐ **Week 49: Align Your Life with Your Soul's Purpose**
  - ○ Poem: The Path Ahead
  - ○ Affirmation: "I align my life with my passion and soul's purpose, creating a reality that fulfills me on every level."
- ☐ **Week 50: Plan for a Future with Self-Love**
  - ○ Poem: Horizon of Self-Love
  - ○ Affirmation: "I move forward with intentions rooted in self-love, confident that my future is bright with possibilities and growth."
- ☐ **Week 51: Create a Vision Board for the Future**
  - ○ Poem: The Bloom Ahead
  - ○ Affirmation: "I look to the future with hope and excitement, knowing that I am fully aligned with my self-love and soul's desires."
- ☐ **Week 52: Reflect and Celebrate Your Growth**
  - ○ Poem: The Garden Grows
  - ○ Affirmation: "I celebrate my growth, my strength, and the love I have cultivated within myself. I honor the work I've done to bloom."

Acknowledgments

Creating *Bloom in Any Season* has been an incredible journey, and I am deeply grateful to the people who have supported, inspired, and guided me along the way.

To my daughter, Meredith Hill, and my family—thank you for your love, encouragement, and unwavering belief in me. Your presence has been my grounding force and your support has carried me through every season of creation and growth. I am endlessly proud of the light and brilliance you each bring into the world.

To Shana Danielle and Nicole Donoho—your coaching and guidance were truly invaluable. Thank you for your wisdom, encouragement, and unwavering support throughout this process. I couldn't have done it without you.

To my incredible clients and friends—your courage, resilience, and dedication to your journeys of growth and self-discovery have been my greatest inspiration. It is an honor to witness and support you as you bloom in your own season.

Finally, thank you to everyone who picks up this book. My hope is that it helps you uncover the magic within, embrace your unfolding, and remember that you are love, you are light, and you are endlessly blessed.

With love and gratitude,
Dr. Makeba

Resources for Growth & Maintenance

This collection of resources is curated to inspire, guide, and support your ongoing journey back to you.

Nourishing Reads: Books

- *"All About Love: New Visions"* by bell hooks – An exploration of love's ability to transform our lives.
- *"The Body Is Not an Apology: The Power of Radical Self-Love"* by Sonya Renee Taylor – Break free from societal confines and water your roots with radical self-love.
- *"The Energy Medicine Solution: Mind Blowing Results for Living an Extraordinary Life"* by Jacqueline Kane – An expert collaboration offering tools to shift, manage, clear, and enhance the energy for your body, mind, soul, and spirit.
- *"Homecoming: A Journey To Light"* by Dr. Makeba Morgan Hill – A collection of poetry chronicling one woman's path of discovery from living, loneliness, lust, and despair to finding love and light within.
- *"Love Warriors: The Conscious Expert's Guide to Healing, Joy, and Manifestation"* by Laura Di Franco
- *"Year of Yes: How to Dance It Out, Stand In the Sun and Be Your Own Person"* by Shonda Rhimes – Learn to bask in your own light by embracing the power of 'yes.'
- *"Vibrate Higher Daily: Live Your Power"* by Lalah Delia – A guide to achieving higher vibrations and embracing one's power through self-care and love.

Enlightenment Through Listening: Podcasts and YouTube

- *"Therapy for Black Girls"* – A sanctuary for nurturing the mental wellness of Black women and girls.
- *"Hey, Girl"* by Alex Elle – Dive deep into conversations about self-care, love, and healing.
- *"Oprah's SuperSoul Conversations"* – Discover life's deeper meanings and how to cultivate a fulfilling existence.

Melodic Growth: Music

- *"Resonance Meditation"* by Beautiful Chorus – Harmonies that inspire peace and a deep feeling of self-love. Perfect for meditation or moments of reflection.
- *"Stay Free"* by Londrelle – Offers a blend of mindfulness, meditation, and self-love. "Stay Free" is an anthem for liberation from within.
- *"I Am Light"* by India.Arie – This song is a reminder of our inner divinity and strength, celebrating the essence of being purely oneself.
- *"Frequency"* by Jhené Aiko – A soothing track that encourages listeners to tune into their own vibrations and elevate their energy through self-care and love.
- *"Brand New Me"* by Alicia Keys – A powerful song about transformation and finding strength in one's own identity, perfect for moments of self-renewal.

Expanding Your Roots: Online Courses and Workshops

- *"The Science of Well-Being"* by Yale University (Coursera) – Equip yourself with the knowledge to tend to your personal happiness.
- *"Strategic Self-Love"* – Join Dr. Makeba in workshop and retreats that provide the tools for planting and nurturing self-love in your life.

Author Bio

Dr. Makeba Morgan Hill is an intuitive personal strategist and spiritual coach based in Atlanta, Georgia. She earned her Bachelor's degree in Healthcare Management from Florida A&M University, a Master of Health Services Administration from George Washington University, and a doctorate in Higher Education from the University of Georgia. With a rich background in strategic planning, Dr. Makeba integrates holistic wellness practices with meticulous strategies to help individuals and organizations realize their fullest potential.

Her work has been featured in holistic wellness publications and she is the author of *Homecoming: A Journey to Light*, a collection of poetry. Renowned for her ability to help others step into their divine mission, Dr. Makeba specializes in unlocking the door to self-discovery, encouraging clients to embrace their intrinsic worth and connect with their higher purpose.

Dr. Makeba enjoys tending to her garden, caring for her cats, and exploring new spiritual practices. Her latest work, *Bloom in Any Season: 52 Ways to Grow into Your Magical Self*, delves into themes of self-love, holistic wellness, and personal growth, offering practical strategies for lasting transformation.

You can learn more about Dr. Makeba and her offerings at www.drmakeba4love.com.

A Special Invitation

Thank you for joining me on this journey! I hope this book has inspired and supported you in your path of self-love, healing, and transformation.

If this book resonated with you, I'd be grateful if you could take two minutes to leave a review on Amazon, letting me know what you thought of the book. Your feedback not only helps others find the book but also helps me improve my future offerings.

If you're ready to take the next step on your journey, I invite you to explore my coaching programs and transformational retreats. Whether you're seeking clarity, confidence, or spiritual alignment, I'd love to support you in stepping into your divine mission.

Learn more at www.drmakeba4love.com and schedule a free strategy session.

With love and gratitude,
Dr. Makeba Morgan Hill